THE FARMING
OF AUSTRALIA

THE FARMING OF AUSTRALIA

A saga of backbreaking toil and tenacity

Robin Bromby

HIGHGATE PUBLISHING - SYDNEY

THE FARMING OF AUSTRALIA

First published 1986 by Doubleday Australia
Re-issued 1989 as UNLOCKING THE LAND by Lothian Books

This expanded and revised edition published 2014 by:
Highgate Publishing
P O Box 481
Edgecliff NSW 2027
Australia www.highgatepublishing.com.au

National Library of Australia Catalogue-in-Publication entry

Bromby, Robin, 1942-
The Farming of Australia: a saga of backbreaking toil and tenacity / Robin Bromby.
3rd ed.

ISBN: 978-0-9874-03827 (Paperback)

Includes bibliographic references.
Agriculture-Australia-History.
630.994

Cover: An iconic image of Australian farming and the bush. Cattle drovers in action.
National Library of Australia.

CONTENTS

A note on imperial measures and currency

In all but roughly the last years covered in this book, the currency of Australia was the pound. And, because of the time scale, conversion to decimal currency is meaningless: for example, paying nine pence for something in 1820 was a substantial sum, unlike 8c in today's money. When this writer began work as a journalist in 1962, he received a weekly wage of around £9 — what sense does it make to render that as $18 in today's money?

The pound consisted of 20 shillings — and each shilling contained 12 pence, and each pound consisted of 144 pence — a system which required a certain mental agility in the years before calculators. To further confuse matters, there were also half-pennies and, in early times, farthings (which were quarter-pennies). When decimal currency arrived in the 1960s, one pound was converted to $2 and shillings became 10c pieces.

In this book, a sum of two pounds, three shillings and seven pence (which today would be $2.37) is rendered as £2 3s 7d. For sums of less than a pound, they were given as either 3s 7d or 3/7.

There was a further complication — guineas. One guinea consisted of £1. 1s — or 21 shillings, as opposed to 20 shillings to the pound. While the guinea coin had long been abandoned in England, it remained as an expression of value in the Antipodes almost to the day of decimal conversion. It had an elitist appeal — a lawyer would send a bill in guineas, a carpenter in pounds.

Other measures:

1 inch   = 25.4mm
1 foot   = 0.3 metres
1 yard   = 0.91 metres
1 mile   = 1.609km
1 square mile = 2.6 square kilometres
1 ton   = 1.01 tonnes
1 gallon = 4.53 litres
1 pound* (weight) = 0.453 kilograms
1 acre** =   0.404 hectares
1 peck = Quarter of a bushel

* designated as "lb"

** An acre is subdivided into roods (1101.7 square metres) and perches (25.29 square metres).

Introduction

Unlocking the land—and its story

In 1911, the Australian agents for Wolseley electric sheep shearing equipment, Dalgety & Co, mounted an impressive display to attract customers.

National Library of Australia.

"WHEN THE NEWSPAPERS publish stories that there are some children in the western suburbs of Sydney who have never seen a cow, or that some Australian children have never eaten fresh vegetables, the yawning gap between town and country is briefly illuminated, as if by a flare on a moonless night, and is just as quickly plunged back into darkness."

In the twenty-six years since I first wrote those words, for the first edition of this book in 1986, the connection between city and country has become ever more tenuous. Back in the 1980s, stories of rural life were still common in the city media. Now the main non-city focus is the resources sector. Even when stories do penetrate the urban consciousness — the live cattle exports to Indonesia being a recent example — it is seen through a prism of city sensibility, in this case animal cruelty. That is not to say that cruelty to any animal is anything but dreadful, but who from the cities raced to the side of the run-holders whose livelihood was eliminated overnight?

The country has its own media ghetto, the farming press. It is there that one reads about the property-by-property accumulation of Australian land by Asian interests; it's there that you have to search to discover that the plight of the dairy farmer is an ongoing story, that the producers are being squeezed more than ever by the large supermarket chains, that debt is still plaguing farmers' lives (average Queensland farm debt having risen by twenty per cent over two years, for example), that the citrus growers of the Riverina have been unable to find markets and so are dumping their fruit for cattle feed.

Whoever in the cities would ever today utter the words "riding on the sheep's back", once the encapsulation of Australian wealth? Now it is coal and iron ore that are seen as the economic saviors.

This situation, therefore, makes it imperative to keep the story alive of the Australian farmer. The reminder of how he (and she) built Australia is needed far more now than in 1986.

And it remains as true today, as then, that a general history of Australian agriculture is a rare beast. The several stages of farming development have separately been chronicled over the past several decades. The squatters and selectors have had their due more than once at the hand of the writer, but it seems that in the majority of works about Australian development of the primary sector, and farming practice in particular, have been dealt with incidentally. The strikes of the 1890s and the gold rushes are possibly more romantic in retrospect than the invention of the stump-jump plough or the conquering of smut in wheat.

Yet the conquering of this island continent is a story, one might argue, of epic proportions. The great debouchment which followed the making of a pass across the Blue Mountains and the subsequent flood of squatters; the great cattle drives to found stations in the Northern Territory and the Kimberley; the pitiful struggle in the wastelands of the Mallee; the work of years being wiped out by drought, often more than once in a lifetime — all this is the stuff of legend and folklore.

This account attempts to portray a broad sweep of one aspect of Australian history — the part of the man and woman on the land. It is not altogether a flattering story. For one thing, ill-advised or just plain ignorant farming practices are a recurring theme. Yet, by sheer perseverance, the Australian agriculturalist and pastoralist have survived in this largely hostile continent. As the first edition of this book was being completed way back in 1986, the sugar-growers of Queensland were facing financial ruin, the dairy farmers of Victoria were blockading dairy factories and shops to fight for greater protection, and the farming community at large was sinking under a mountain of debt and high costs, suggesting only — as I wrote then — that the next decades were going to be no less difficult than the ones which preceded them.

Since then, of course, we have had another terrible drought but the farming community is still there, under threat as ever.

Now we have a new concern not even contemplated back in 1986: the spectre of an agricultural country no longer able to be self-sustaining. We now import a third of our fruit and twenty per cent of our vegetables. And we continue to lose prime agricultural land: the depredations of coal-seam gas and open-cast coal mining are just the latest threats to our agricultural industry.

Droughts we can live through. Low market prices can be endured. But the loss — forever — of farming land is not a story with a happy ending.

Chapter 1

A Miserable Beginning

Braidswood, New South Wales. The dairy at Anderson's farm on the Clyde Road.

National Library of Australia

THE FIRST FARMS in Australia were sorry affairs. James Atkinson, who left one of the earliest accounts of agricultural life in New South Wales, described the state of farming in 1826 as 'rude and miserable'. That the first farmers in the new colony at Sydney were frequently unable to grow enough to feed the tiny population was not surprising, considering that they came largely from the ranks of emancipated convicts and had little or no knowledge of the rudiments of farming. Of the earliest convict settlers, Atkinson wrote that 'a more improvident, worthless race of people, cannot well be imagined'.

Early attempts at taming the land

Governor Phillip was the first to attempt to cultivate the Australian soil, with nine acres set aside at Farm Cove, now the site of the Sydney Botanical Gardens. His ambition was to make the new settlement self-supporting with minimal capital. Not that he had much choice; the First Fleet had arrived with one bull, one bull calf, four cows, one stallion, three mares, three colts, forty-four sheep, four goats, twenty-eight pigs, some fowl and turkeys and a small miscellaneous collection of plants and seeds. His optimism regarding the land's potential was based on an overly enthusiastic report compiled by Sir Joseph Banks for a committee of the House of Commons; the soil around Sydney and Farm Cove was too sandy to provide the food that was obviously going to be needed. In a despatch of 15 May 1788, Phillip reported to London that eight acres were to be planted with wheat and barley but he feared much of that would be ruined by mice and ants. There was also the problem of clearing the bush. There were no work-horses and the convicts were, by and large, lazy and ignorant. In 1789, out of a total of 750 convicts, only a third were engaged in farming.

Phillip came quickly to the conclusion that free settlers, with the proper tools and a knowledge of farming, were essential. In June 1790, he wrote to the British government:

> Settlers appear to me to be absolutely necessary. If they bring with them people to clear and cultivate the land, and provisions to support those who bring them, they will want for very little assistance from government after they arrive; but no soldier, or other person in this settlement, could at present accept of the assistance of convicts in cultivating the land which might be granted them ... I believe, Sir, that it will be little less than two years from the time of granting the lands, before those lands will support the cultivators.

It had become increasingly obvious to Philip that, without the enterprise of the free settlers, training in stock raising and proper crop management, the colony would always be partially dependent on supplies from Britain.

Not only were the convicts intransigent in their ignorance, but their gaolers had to deal with a strange climate where the seasons were upside down, the rainfall was uncertain and hot winds besieged Sydney for days at a time. Despair was all that flourished, exacerbated by the knowledge that the home authorities were largely indifferent to the comfort of their exiled subjects and were cruelly disregarding the suffering reported to them. The crops languished in the sandy soil and — as if all else were not enough — the bull and cows disappeared, not to be found until 1795, by which time they had prospered in the wild and grown to a herd of more than forty.

By May 1790, the settlers were desperate. They faced the very real prospect of starvation. The greatest crime was to steal food: one man detected filching potatoes was given 300 lashes, chained to other convicts for six months and suffered the loss of his flour ration.

Phillip dispatched ships to Batavia and India to purchase and load urgently needed rice, wheat and other grain, but in February 1790 the colony's storehouse had only enough food left to cover four months, and that had been calculated on the basis of half-rations. Another blow was the sinking of the vessel *Guardian* at the Cape of Good Hope while it was bringing stores to Sydney. The arrival of the Second Fleet did mean that stores were replenished, but there was also many more mouths to feed. In April 1790, the colonists were limited to a weekly ration of just over four pounds of flour, a pound and a half of rice and two and a half pounds of pork.

Again and again Phillip asked for genuine English farmers to be sent out as no one seemed to know or care anything about the work. The lack of rain complicated matters, as Phillip wrote in November 1790:

> I do not think that all the showers of the last four months put together would make twenty-four hours' rain. Our farms, what with this and the poor soil, are in wretched condition. My winter crop of potatoes, which I planted in days of despair, turned out very badly when I dug them two months back.

It was the first of many droughts which the settlers had to face. In 1791 no substantial rain fell between June and November. All public work was suspended at one stage because the convicts were not capable of hard labouring. They were on short rations, and were enervated by the heat. Phillip reported to London, in a letter dated October 1791, that there had scarcely been a drop of rain in sixteen weeks.

The Governor had quickly seen the need to locate good farming land if the young settlement was to be self-supporting. He searched Broken Bay, the Hawkesbury and Parramatta rivers for the best land. On 2 November 1788 he decided upon Rose Hill (now the city of Parramatta). After establishing a forty-acre government farm there, Phillip developed plans to allow sentence-expired convicts to have farms of their own. By the end of November the first such sentence-expired convict, James Ruse, was allowed to occupy and cultivate land at Parramatta on his own account.

When Phillip left New South Wales in 1792 he had established sixty-eight settlers on small farms located in clusters at Parramatta, Prospect Hill, Kissing Point, Northern Boundary and the Ponds and Field of Mars.

Ruse can be said to be Australia's first white farmer. In a letter to London Phillip described the ex-convict's efforts:

> In order to know in what time a man might be able to cultivate a sufficient quantity of ground to support himself, I last November ordered a hut to be built in a good situation, an acre of land to be cleared and once turned up. It was put in possession of a very industrious convict, who was told if he behaved well he should have thirty acres. He has been industrious, has received some little assistance from time to time, and now tells me that if one acre more is cleared for him he shall be able to support himself after next January, which I much doubt, but think he will do tolerably well after he has been supported for eighteen months. Others may prove more intelligent, though they cannot be more industrious.

Ruse, who had been born in Cornwall and raised on a farm, later described his methods of clearing the land at Parramatta: after felling the trees, he burned them on the ground, and then dug in the ashes. He then proceeded to clod-mould the soil and dig in grass and weeds, letting it all lie as long as possible exposed to air and sun, turning it over just before he sowed.

> When I shall have reaped my crop, I propose to hoe it again and harrow it fine and then sow it with turnip seed, which will mellow and prepare it for next year. My straw I mean to bury in pits and throw in with it everything which I think will rot and turn to manure.

Within four months, Ruse had his thirty acres, the first such grant in Australia. It was aptly named Experiment Farm, and was to pass through many forms, including a Chinese market garden, before being overtaken by housing development. Ruse has been described as inward-looking, not particularly sociable and a loner.

By the time Ruse had reaped his first crop in 1790, the food situation had marginally improved. In June ships arrived with provisions, and by the end of the year Phillip was able to report that 200 acres had been cleared and cultivated at Rose Hill. The harvest that year amounted to 200 bushels of wheat, sixty bushels of barley, a small quantity of flax, Indian corn and oats, all of which were preserved for seed. A year later the Public Gardener, David Burton, compiled a list for the Governor which showed the amount of land under cultivation at Parramatta:

ACRES	ROODS	PERCHES	
351	2	5	Maize
44	1	8	Wheat
6	1	30	Barley
1	—	—	Oats
2	—	3	Potatoes
4	2	—	Not cultivated, but cleared
4	2	15	Crescent, mostly planted with vines
6	—	—	Governor's garden, partly sowed with maize and wheat
80	—	—	Garden ground belonging to individuals
17	—	—	Land cultivated by N.S.W. Corps
150	—	—	Cleared, to be sowed in turnips
91	3	2	Ground in cultivation by settlers
28	—	—	Ground in cultivation by civil and military officers
134	—	—	Enclosed, and the timber thinned for feeding cattle.

Burton added, by way of comment, that the crops were generally light owing to lack of rain. In July 1792 several ships arrived at Port Jackson from the Cape of Good Hope and India bringing supplies, so that once again the settlers were issued with full rations. These consisted of four pounds of maize, three pounds of soujee, six pounds of beef and quantities of peas and rice. A mere thirteen days' supply of flour was left in the government stores when the ship Atlantic arrived from Bengal that year. But the relief was temporary, and food shortages continued to plague New South Wales for more than a decade. In 1796, famine was averted only by the enterprising efforts of the officers and the food they were able to produce from their cultivations. In 1800 salt was rationed; in 1801 pork rations were cut. As late as 1807, Governor Bligh reported the dispatch of a brig to China for rice. He did not expect it to return for eight months, commenting: 'We must, therefore, struggle through until the next harvest, which will teach the settlers to be more provident and industrious than by any admonition whatever'.

Too few of the settlers, even the free ones, had more than a superficial knowledge of farming. With the convicts, there was not much hope.

Governor King noted crisply that it was impossible to make farmers out of London pickpockets. By the same token, it was hardly surprising that the convicts showed little will to work: they had no desire to be in Australia, and they had little or no faith that anything much could be made out of what they saw as a hostile land. They had been brought to Australia by force, and were given inadequate tools with which to cultivate the land.

Poor seed was a constant problem, and the crops could hardly be expected to thrive when the land was sown with the same seed year after year. Farming was often so slovenly that corn crops were grown in the same field as the previous year's crop without any intervening green crop to clear the land. Different varieties of seed were mixed together, with the result that the crop would ripen at different stages depending on the variety of the corn or wheat seed. The waste of wheat and corn was consequently considerable. Barley, which King encouraged in order to provide the basis for beer brewing and thus cut spirit consumption (a forlorn hope, as it turned out) suffered similarly at the hands of those who cultivated the land. The only crops which seemed to thrive were turnips and tobacco.

Another early visitor to New South Wales, James Bonwick, recorded some of the other handicaps to good farming. Bengal cattle turned out to be bad milkers, many of the horses were badly bred, and the sheep often had coarse hair more usually found on goats. If these early Australian farmers could not figure out proper cultivation procedures, then planned stock breeding was hardly likely to feature among their accomplishments.

By contrast, the cattle which had escaped in the early months of the settlement had done very nicely for themselves. They had made their way up the Nepean River, some forty miles beyond Parramatta. By 1800, the herd had grown in number to about 300 and by 1810 there were 5,000 head. They were still wild, but had been declared to be the government herd. The cattle had been accidentally discovered by two convicts in 1795, whereupon Governor Hunter set off up country to see them for himself. The country in which the cattle were found was described in a contemporary account as 'remarkably pleasant to the eye'. Trees were thinly scattered and the ground covered in luxuriant pasture, with large ponds upon which ducks and black swan swam. Hunter foresaw the day when the cattle would provide a continuing source of fresh meat and placed them under his protection. That was still some time away; even in 1807 a full year's supply of meat had to be shipped from London to the struggling colonists. Meanwhile, the stock in the possession of the civil and military officers and the government had been increasing slowly. The count on 1 September 1796 showed fifty-seven mares and horses, 101 cows and cow-calves, seventy-four bulls and bull-calves, fifty-two oxen, more than 1,500 sheep, 1,400 goats and 1,800 hogs. Land under cultivation totalled 5,410 acres. The colony's figures in August 1799 reveal the progress made: the number of horses and mares had doubled, bulls and oxen were rapidly increasing, cows had increased five-fold; there were more than 5,000 sheep, 2,763 goats and 3,459 hogs. Six thousand acres were planted in wheat, 2,500 acres in maize, with barley, oats and potatoes in addition. The agricultural efforts of the officers made a considerable impact on the early development of New South Wales. But it was James Macarthur who showed that money was to be made.

Macarthur was granted a block of land adjoining Ruse's Experiment Farm. In 1794 his 247 acres, of which 100 were under cultivation, produced an income of £400. Then he re-sowed twenty acres in wheat and eighty acres in Indian corn and potatoes. The following year, his wife wrote home that there were nearly 120 acres planted in wheat, and that there was an abundance of fruit and vegetables. She recorded that Macarthur had built his cattle herd to fifty and that his sheep numbered 1,000. Yet they had not slaughtered any of the sheep for meat because of Macarthur's interest in producing wool, nor did they take all the milk produced, as some of it was kept for calf-rearing. He was the first settler to use a plough drawn by oxen. Macarthur and his fellow members of the New South Wales Corps were quick to take advantage of their land grants. By 1796 they owned thirty-one per cent of the cultivated land and more than three-quarters of the livestock in private hands. Macarthur's contribution to Australia was his work with wool, a commodity not greatly prized in the earliest days of New South Wales.

He had arrived in 1790, aged twenty-three, and £500 in debt. Eleven years later he was a man of substance, although Governor King's estimate that Macarthur was worth £20,000 was in all probability a gross exaggeration. Macarthur's fortune was made possible by his position in the New South Wales Corps which gave him (and others) the opportunity to buy cargoes of rum and resell them to the settlers at enormous profit. This commercial shrewdness was a natural advantage when it came to acquiring blocks of land beyond the initial 100 acres granted. He managed to parlay his original stake largely by shrewd agriculture.

Unlike most other farmers raising sheep in the colony, he was more interested in wool than meat. He was not the first to import merino sheep, but he was one of the first to cross-breed them in an attempt to produce an improved fleece. When Macarthur was sent to England in 1801 to face a court-martial for duelling with another officer he met the leaders of the English textile industry. Anxious to obtain a substitute supply of wool after shipments from Germany and Spain had been interrupted by the Napoleonic Wars, they showed interest in Macarthur's samples of his new improved fleeces. Their encouraging response was enough to spur him to buy nine rams and a ewe from the King's merino flock at Kew.

By order of the British Government, Macarthur was given a large tract of 10,000 acres on his return to Sydney in 1805. The land was situated at Cowpastures, where the original small herd of 1788 had flourished in the wild.

A year later Governor Bligh sailed through the heads into Sydney Harbour, intent to impose his own view of law and order. Bligh and Macarthur soon clashed violently, largely because of Bligh's determined efforts to break the rum monopoly. This fight, which led to rebellion and the overthrow of the governor, forced Macarthur to live in England for several years to avoid prosecution for treason. While his wife Elizabeth ran the farms, Macarthur learned about the textile trade and the problems involved in trying to sell wool to England. In 1817, when he was allowed to return to Australia without the risk of prosecution, his farms were flourishing. By this time he owned more than 5,000 sheep, but the colony had grown too large for him to dominate as he had in the previous decade. Nevertheless, when John Thomas Bigge compiled his influential report on farming in New South Wales in 1823, he was able to extol Macarthur's role. This gave support to the Australian Agricultural Company which Macarthur floated the following year with £1 million in capital.

Bigge's report was hardly fair to those besides Macarthur who had the imagination to see what could lie before them in the colony. A fellow officer, Captain Waterhouse, had also attempted to build up a merino flock and, in fact, sold Macarthur sheep before the turn of the century. The Reverend Samuel Marsden was described by Governor King as the best practical farmer in the colony, although that may merely have been intended to snub Macarthur. Marsden acquired land in 1802 at what is now St Mary's and within two years had established a flock of 1,200 sheep. Like Macarthur he was interested in breeding and in 1807 took his first samples of wool to England. By the time of his death in 1838 Marsden and his family had acquired land as far away as Molong in the Central West of New South Wales.

The life of the 'Dungaree' settlers

James Atkinson provided a vivid description of the manner in which the early settlers made themselves a home. First they cut down a few trees, set up saplings as corner posts and then formed a roof frame with small poles. The walls and the roof were filled with slabs of bark, a space was left for a door and a square hole cut for a window. Both openings were covered at night. Long pieces, lined with turf to prevent them catching fire, formed a chimney at one end of this rude structure. These huts were surprisingly long-lasting, some having been continuously inhabited for twenty years by the time Atkinson set down his account. Platforms of bark acted as beds and tables, with blocks being used as chairs. The typical hut was furnished with blankets and mattresses, with a few bags being kept to hold clothes, flour, tea and sugar. The better-off settlers owned a mill and a sieve for grinding the wheat into flour. These people were commonly known as 'Dungaree Settlers', a name which derived from the coarse Indian cloth used to fashion their garments.

In spite of all the problems, a few individuals showed the colony could provide a comfortable and prosperous life if the effort were made. Major Francis Grose, who arrived in 1792 as Phillip's Lieutenant Governor, expressed surprise at the fertility of the gardens surrounding his house. 'Vegetables are here in great abundance, and I live in as good a house as I wish for', he wrote to London.

Surrounded by a kitchen garden and vineyard, the Macarthurs' house was single-storeyed and included servant's quarters. Mrs Macarthur wrote:

> We fatten and kill a great number of hogs in the year, which enables us to feed a large establishment of servants. The labourers are such as have been convicts, and whose time of transportation has expired.

Not everyone valued convict labour. In 1793 Major Grose, having taken over from Phillip, complained about the convicts who had been freed and given land. 'I am much plagued with the people who become settlers and who have evidently no other view than the purpose of raising a sufficient supply to pay their passage to England,' he noted in a dispatch dated 9 January 1793. It was only after Phillip departed that Grose, anxious to increase the quantity of food produced in the colony, allotted land to the officers, then to other ranks — so setting the foundation for several private fortunes, such as that of John Macarthur.

Free settlers turn to farming

While of a later era than early settlement, this photograph of a boundary rider's home at May Downs, Queensland, illustrates how, for many decades, the poorer of country workers lived in very rudimentary conditions.

John Oxley Library.

The free settlers were not much better farmers than the emancipated convicts.

The first lot arrived aboard the *Bellona* in January 1793 and established themselves on land at Homebush and Strathfield, then known as Liberty Plains. The productive capacity of the land selected by these settlers was quickly exhausted by overcropping, so that the farmers had to keep clearing land for their fields. This process served only to keep them in a continual state of poverty, sinking deeper into debt and scrounging what credit they could.

Although the Parramatta area was flood-free and closer to the markets, the eyes of the colonial administrators started to turn toward the Hawkesbury River. Ruse, who had sold up at Rose Hill for £40, was allowed to move with twenty-six other farmers to the Hawkesbury, where they began to clear land near the present town of Windsor. At the end of December 1797 Governor Hunter sailed up the river to visit the new settlement. He reminded the settlers that they were still considerably indebted to the government for the seed from which their crops were produced.

He was later to remark on the folly of the settlers in cultivating the low lands on the Hawkesbury when there had been sufficient evidence that it was subject to flooding. The Hawkesbury grants had been first issued by Grose and this policy was continued, first by Governor Hunter, and then by King, who allowed the settlers more than the previous limit of thirty acres. John Bigge, reporting to the House of Commons, said that the occupiers of the smaller tracts appeared to be in a state of abject poverty; much of which was due to the floods, which first struck in 1799. Earlier that year the continued drought had played havoc with the crops: the wheat proved little better than chaff and the maize was shrivelled on the ground. It was the worst period of drought since the First Fleet had arrived. Writing to the Duke of Portland in June, Hunter stated that there had been no rain for ten months, the streams had dried up and the country was a blaze of fire.

Then the rains came.

The settlers who had built their homes and planted their crops on the low-lying land were inundated. One man was drowned and all the crops were lost. Bigge wrote in 1823 that Governor Macquarie had on a number of occasions tried to persuade the settlers of the Hawkesbury to repair to high lands on the opposite banks of the river where the land was above the flood levels, 'but either from inability to construct new habitations, or from unwillingness to leave their old ones, the lower class of settler have, in very few instances, taken advantage of these offers.' Considering the number of floods in those early years this is surprising. Floods occurred in March 1806 (when the river rose eighty-eight feet and £30,000 worth of goods were destroyed), in March 1808, 1811, June 1816, March 1817, February 1819 and October 1820. The floods were particularly serious when they occurred in March, as was often the case, because at that time of the year the farmers were either preparing the ground for wheat or had paddocks of ripening maize. The continued cultivation of the land resulted in wheat yields falling by more than forty per cent for the early 1820s.

The usual first crop for the settler breaking in a block of land was maize, planted in October. While it grew the farmer would spend his time building fences around his land, using boughs and brushwood. Then he would earth and hill his maize, later felling and burning off more land to take wheat. The maize would be ready in March or April. The cobs were then gathered in, put in a loft, and the stalks pulled up and burned. The ground was broadcast sown in wheat which, provided all went well, was ready in November for harvesting. Immediately the wheat was harvested the farmer planted stubble corn or maize, and the process was repeated in the following years. Hence the soil was exhausted. It was a situation which irritated Atkinson, who wrote:

> The settlers of this class have seldom any livestock, except perhaps a few pigs and poultry; no manure is therefore made upon the farm, and it is common

practice to burn the straw and corn stalks; this, I am sorry to say, I have
frequently seen done upon farms where better things might be expected ...
many of the finest tracts were thus ruined and exhausted.

Inevitably the creditors seized the land when a farmer was no longer able to
pay his debts. These creditors were often ex-convicts who, by cunning, managed
to come into possession of a great deal of land. The final humiliation for the
settlers was then to be employed on what had been their own land.

Atkinson reported there were settlers who had sufficient capital, but even
among these there were plenty who lacked agricultural knowledge and skill.
He looked after his livestock with care, allowing three oxen for each plough,
working two at a time so that one was always resting.

A somewhat more glossy report about the state of affairs in New South Wales
was given in the *Edinburgh Farmer's Magazine* in 1820 by W.C. Wentworth.
This most famous of the squatters suggested that, in terms of fertility, the banks
of the Nepean could be compared with those of the Nile. Somewhat at variance
with other contemporary accounts, Wentworth reported that the average yield
of maize on the river banks of the Nepean and Hawkesbury was a bountiful
eighty to 100 bushels per acre, and of wheat between thirty and forty bushels
per acre.

A report by Dangar in 1828 published in London gives a different picture:
that wheat was subject to the same diseases and failures which hit the crop in
England but that maize generally grew much better. English barley averaged
thirty bushels an acre but only a small quantity was required for malting; oats
were found to ripen prematurely in the heat; peas were a sure and productive
crop but were grown only for domestic purposes; turnips were not extensively
cultivated as they were not so essential to stock fattening as in the English
winter; and rape was exceedingly productive. Of the grasses, the best adapted
to the climate were Dutch clover, lucerne, meadow-fescue, rib grass and burnet.
At this time the curing of hay was exceedingly profitable within reasonable
transport distance of Sydney.

As New South Wales reached the twentieth year of European settlement,
a farming population was beginning to establish itself in Tasmania, or Van
Diemen's Land as it was then known. King had been alarmed by reports reaching
Sydney that the French were considering establishing a base at Storm Bay, near
the present site of Hobart. The French vessels *Geographe* and *Naturaliste* had
visited the island in 1801. The last thing the British Government wanted was
French expansion in the South Seas in the middle of the Napoleonic wars. King
hurriedly despatched John Bowen, a very young naval lieutenant, to establish
a base on the Derwent. Lieutenant-Colonel Paterson was shortly afterwards

sent to found a settlement on the north coast of Tasmania, at Port Dalrymple. Bowen was superseded the next year when Lieutenant Colonel David Collins arrived, having abandoned efforts to settle at Port Phillip Bay. He decided to move the settlement organised by Bowen to the banks of the Derwent in early 1804 and parcelled out land in 100 acre lots for the settlers at New Town Bay. In 1810 Oxley, a visitor to the new colony, recorded the scene at New Town Bay:

> White cottages in the midst of tolerable good gardens afford a pleasing contrast to the wilderness of the surrounding scenery. The ground here is either fit for tillage or grazing, but the settlers have not made the most of their situation; few of them originally were farmers or understood anything of agriculture; they have in consequence so exhausted their ground by repeated crops of the same grain that it produces little or nothing.

A familiar tale in early Australia!

In fact, the first convicts in Tasmania were as reluctant to become farmers as were their counterparts at Sydney, while the free settlers were often ignorant of good farming practices. By July 1804 it was reported that the ground in cultivation around Hobart consisted of twenty acres of wheat, two acres in oats and in rye. Again, as in Sydney, many of the settlers placed more value on liquor than they did on land. Nor did they have sufficient horses or oxen. The main instrument of tillage was the hoe, which was a slow enough instrument without the further handicap of being used by unpractised hands. The nascent colony was completely dependent upon food shipments from Sydney but these ceased as a result of the floods on the Hawkesbury in 1806. The new Tasmanians were left to their own devices.

The substitute was kangaroo meat, and for some years the kangaroo hunters were the colony's chief suppliers of food. Just as Phillip had been unwilling to insist on convicts toiling at public works when food was short, so Collins had to allow convicts on the Derwent freedom to search for food, thus laying the foundation for the bushranger era which sorely tried the early governors of Tasmania. The colonists were further disappointed when a ship sent to India for wheat sank.

Oxley's impression was confirmed by John West, who wrote his classic history of Tasmania in 1852. He recorded the sight of unfenced fields of grain, deformed with blackened stumps. The typical farm he saw had a low cottage of the meanest structure, surrounded by heaps of wool, bones and sheepskins. Mutton and kangaroo meat were strung up in trees. Idle and dirty men hung about.

Again, Wentworth gave a glowing report for the benefit of potential migrants back in Britain. The greatest asset, he wrote, was that land was free of timber:

> There the colonist has no expense to incur in clearing his farm; he is not compelled to a great preliminary outlay of capital before he can expect a considerable return; he has only to set fire to the grass, to prepare his land for the immediate reception of the ploughshare: so that if he but possess a good team of horses, or oxen, with a set of harness, and a couple of substantial ploughs, he has the main requisite for commencing an agricultural establishment.

How easy he made it all sound.

The settlement at Port Dalrymple was fortunate to have Paterson. He was a keen botanist and was greatly interested in farming. It was he who introduced livestock into Tasmania. In 1805 a shipment of 612 cows arrived from Bengal, and the next year he landed 200 sheep from Macarthur's flocks, so setting the stage for Tasmania's wool exports. The first wool was exported from Tasmania in 1819. Tasmania's Agriculture Society was formed in the early 1820s, giving rise to one of the earliest recorded instances of inter-colonial sniping, exchanges to become such an integral and diverting element in Australian life. One Thomas Kent was moved in 1824 to publish a public letter to Barron Field who, as president of the Agricultural Society of New South Wales, had seen fit to make a few remarks about Van Diemen's Land the previous year. Among his assertions were the statements that fine wool could not be produced in Van Diemen's Land's cold climate, that all the cleared land was already accounted for, that there was insufficient land for grazing, and that the country was badly watered and the cattle and sheep had to be winter foddered. Kent's letter, needless to say, went to some lengths to disprove the attack from the north.

By about 1820, the colony of New South Wales was beginning to outgrow its initial stage. The officer class was no longer dominant. The free settlers were in such numbers by then that a new gentry class was emerging. It was quite apparent, too, that the colony could not go on relying on a continuing inflow of convicts to provide cheap labour. The colony had to establish its own independent economy. When the Agricultural Society was formed on 5 July 1822, its regulations and prospectus stated:

> It becomes us therefore to provide for ourselves; to make the most of the land we have cleared; to improve our fleeces, our horses and our milch cattle; to look out for new exports; to improve the present; to distil our own grain, and to grow our own tobacco.

What is believed to have been the first co-operative established in Australia: the Bergalia Co-op Dairy Co Ltd, located on the south coast of New South Wales.

National Library of Australia.

The growth was impressive. In 1808, figures compiled in Sydney showed the areas under cultivation: wheat 6,877 acres, maize 3,389 acres, barley 544 acres, oats 92 acres, peas and beans 100 acres, potatoes 301 acres, turnips 13 acres, orchards 546 acres and flax and hemp covered 34 acres. (By 1850, there were 491,000 acres being cultivated in the Australian colonies — 198,000 acres in New South Wales, 169,000 in Tasmania and 52,190 acres in Victoria.) Sydney was still the centre of the colonist's world in the first decades of European settlement of New South Wales. Most settlers lived within a radius of about forty miles of Macquarie Street, but the outward thrust was about to begin. In 1822 two merchants, Alexander Berry and Edward Wollstonecraft, established themselves on 13,500 acres at the mouth of the Shoalhaven River. Settlers began moving north to the Hunter Valley where they could dispatch their produce down the river and then by sea to Sydney. The grasses of the country around what was to be Bathurst beckoned the sheep farmer, while in the Illawarra region the land was highly suited to raising and fattening cattle.

The population of the colony was still small, but now it had new horizons.

Chapter 2

Everything on Four Feet

It is shearing time near Brewarrina in northern New South Wales c. 1890. Note the rudimentary fencing.

National Library of Australia

SINCE GOVERNOR Phillip looked up from Sydney Cove and sought new pastures inland, the story of Australia's development has been one of the gradual extension of the outer lines of settlement. The pace of this development has varied according to the mood of the time, whether it was one of optimism in boom years or of tentativeness in depression. Progress has been checked only by natural disaster, but in the long run it was inexorable.

So, for all the travails of the new colony of Sydney, not least of which was the precarious state of food supply even twenty years after the arrival of the

First Fleet , the settlers were ready to break out of their coastal confines. In 1814 convicts were detailed to build a road across the Blue Mountains to open up the vast hinterland. The spread of farming to the banks of the Hawkesbury River had been the first foray away from the coast, but the movement of stock across the Blue Mountains was a giant leap forward. This was to be followed quickly by the race of pastoralist squatters to the Murrumbidgee in the south and to what is now Bourke in the northwest; the later but similar waves in Queensland and Victoria, and the raging optimism of the South Australians pushing into the desert fringes. Yet it was not until the 1880s—100 years after the First Fleet—that the present pattern of close settlement of Australia's usable countryside began, a process made possible by the railway.

The discovery of gold a few decades after the initial expansion provided a dramatic infusion of wealth into the Australian colonies, just as oil and mineral finds in the 1960s and 1970s justified the 'lucky country' tag. However, agricultural and pastoral production was the base and mainstay of the Australian economy even after the gold boom of the 1850s and beyond; sheep and their wool gave Australia its first export produce of any size. The resources developments from the 1960s saw a competing economic pillar begin to emerge and this has continued to expand its influence in the decades since. Now when you talk of the "two-speed economy", it is resources versus the rest, farming being lumped in with all other non-resources sectors.

The expansion of settlement had been made possible in 1813 when Gregory Blaxland, William Wentworth and William Lawson made the first crossing of the Blue Mountains, after which the road was built and the town of Bathurst founded by Governor Macquarie. Within the next five years, the land as far as the Lachlan and Castlereagh rivers, and the tablelands of New England, became known to the colonists.

In 1829, the unpopular Governor Darling had issued an order that no grazing could take place farther than 150 miles from Sydney. But it was too late. Hume had already, on separate journeys, reached Port Phillip Bay and, with Charles Sturt , the lower reaches of the Murray River. When Thomas Mitchell, Surveyor-General of New South Wales, penetrated what is now Victoria to Portland Bay in the west, he found that the Henty family had already travelled from Van Diemen's Land and established themselves at there, unbeknown to the authorities of either colony. In 1827 and 1828 Allan Cunningham had explored the Darling Downs in what was later to be Queensland.

In 1832 a licence fee of five shillings (later increased to twelve, then £1) was levied for Crown land, but neither licensing nor Darling's order could prevent the land-hungry pushing into the uncharted interior. These prospective pastoralists assembled as great a flock as they could afford and a quantity of supplies (also limited by financial resources) and then simply set off from Sydney to walk as far as they need in order to secure their own piece of land. After the climb over the rude road passing across the Blue Mountains, they faced endless plains interspersed with rivers and marshlands, all traversed under the hot relentless sun. It was by no means certain that these settlers would find unoccupied land suited to farming or even live long enough to do so, but there was no room for doubt and indecision. Nothing mattered but land. While they were relieved by the discovery that stock need not be housed in the winter in this new land, that relief was far outweighed by the twin tyrannies of distance and drought. The historian Stephen Roberts likened the thrust into the hinterland to a protoplasm which is for a time retarded but then suddenly grows rapidly to make up for the previous delay. That later stage, he said, came in 1835 when free immigration began in earnest and the old predominance of the convicts (and emancipists) was being threatened.

For the first time, the concept of Australia being confined to Sydney and Hobart Town was being swept away and a greater vision taking its place. Disregarding the restrictions that Darling had placed on them, the settlers were interested only in pasture for their flocks and herds. By 1834 Tamworth had been reached and established.

The magic word was wool

The dream portrayed by Macarthur and others had, by all appearances, reached its fulfilment. Roberts wrote:

> Nobody minded being called a 'squatter' now, bitter reproach though that term had been even a year before, and rational persons thought of the 'squatters' now as persons to be encouraged. The mania was in full swing, and every able-bodied man thirsted for the bush and pined to ride in the dust behind masses of smelling sheep and live on an unchanging diet of mutton-chops, unleavened damper and post-and-rail tea. It was something in men's blood ... Thus the little community of 70,000 dreamed and speculated, and thus sheep, too often ridden with scab and catarrh, set the tone of everything. It was a curiously topsy-turvy time, with men's perspectives strangely blunted. The bush, sheep, the clipper on the tide-the process ran almost like a refrain in men's minds, and the community sang their song of the western waggon and turned towards the interior.
>
> —*The Squatting Age in Australia* by Stephen Roberts, 1935

Macarthur's enterprise in exporting wool to Britain, and being able to interest the textile merchants and clothiers as to its potential advantages over that produced on the Continent, was helped along by two events. First, as mentioned already, there was the prolonged war with Napoleon and its disruption of the previously steady supply of wool from Europe. Secondly, the work of Macarthur and other visionaries had led to a consciousness of the importance of sheep-breeding among the squattocracy.

Not that the trade was without its setbacks. Although by 1830 the standard of wool being exported had improved dramatically, the economic depression in England between 1825 and 1829 had severe repercussions on the income of the Australian pastoralists. When the French were defeated and peace and trade restored throughout Europe not only did the supply of competing wool resume — which by itself could have easily brought an end to the expanding Australian exports — but the German states began selling fine wools at such a low price that English farmers themselves, even with increased tariff protection, could not sustain the competition. What hope then for the Australians 10,000 miles away? With all that and the English economic crisis, Southdown wool, which in 1815 had sold for two and sixpence a pound, was down to a wretched ninepence by 1827.

About 6,000 sheep being driven through the streets of Charleville, Queensland in 1956, bound for the railway station to be loaded on wagons bound for Brisbane. Queensland law required that sheep being driven on roads travel at least ten miles a day.

National Library of Australia

Yet the trade survived. In 1826, Australian growers sent more than a million pounds weight of wool to the London market. By 1839 Van Diemen's Land and New South Wales exported more than ten million pounds of wool to England. The impact of Australian wool on the English market can be seen clearly by looking at the percentage of that market it was able to secure. In 1810 it was a tiny 3.8 per cent, crawling up to 8.1 per cent by 1830, and then exploding, more than doubling, to 22 per cent a decade later. The dramatic rise of Australian wool exports is shown in relief by the comparative figures of Britain's wool imports:

Country of Origin	1815	1844
Spain	6,927,934 lbs	127,559 lbs
Germany	3,137,438 lbs	12,750,011 lbs
Australia	73,171 lbs	35,879,171 lbs

By 1849 there were almost 16 million sheep in Australia. Wool made Australia a solvent nation.

A better class of squatter

By this time, too, as Roberts says, the term 'squatter' had lost its earlier pejorative flavour. Many of the early land-grabbers managed to prosper by the simple expedient of theft — theft of stock and goods of all kind. The spark of free immigration brought a better class of squatter. Instead of the emancipist who might (or might not) have become a reformed character as a result of the chastening experience of transportation, there came from the British Isles a large number of untainted settlers, some of them even with farming experience. This migration and the advent of large-scale squatting inevitably swung the balance of power from the 'pure merinos' (the Macarthur party) to the new men, and the governors had to recognise that. Once there were enough of the land-hungry there was safety in numbers; they could simply set themselves up on a piece of land. It soon became clear that the flouted restrictions on settlement could no longer be defended in Sydney, for the simple reason that the majority of the population was opposed to them. The force for change became irresistible.

Bourke, who had followed Darling at Government House, had recognised this with his system of annual licences, but no one on an annual licence was going to make any improvements. Then John Batman had sailed across Bass Strait from Van Diemen's Land to settle at Port Phillip Bay. The Government recognised the inevitable and, in 1836, threw that district open to settlement, just a year after the *Sydney Gazette* had been complaining that squatting implanted 'the seeds of vice, ignorance and reckless roving'. Ben Boyd arrived with £200,000 to invest on behalf of English speculators. Former officers and sons of the Sydney gentry were all joining the rush for land.

Bourke's licence fee was charged regardless of the size of the holding or the stock upon it. On the Liverpool Plains, eight leases covered 1. 7 million acres. One of the problems faced by the government in Sydney was the difficulty of knowing exactly what was happening throughout the vast hinterland being opened up with such lightning speed. Mitchell's discovery of the Hentys at Portland, where they had been farming undetected for six years, was ample proof of the problem. In fact, the early squatters took great care to locate their primitive stations well away from the main tracks of travellers.

The Henry Hepwood punt at Echuca, Victoria, at the crossing of the River Murray. Punts and pontoon bridges were essential before standing bridges were built.

National Library of Australia

Early life in the colony

One such traveller who left a graphic account of the scenes up country was Annabella Boswell. On a trip down to Liverpool by bullock dray in 1839, her sharp eye caught the scene at a place called Water Holes, an overnight camping spot for the many dray teams working the road. Some drays were on their way to Sydney groaning under heavy loads of wool bales, others returning to their stations carrying supplies for the year ahead. Describing the scene, Annabella Boswell wrote:

> It really was astonishing to see some of the large wool drays and how they were packed, and often on the top of all was to be seen a woman and two or three small children. How they got up was a mystery to me, and being up, how they travelled on such roads and met with so few accidents was still more wonderful. Each dray was drawn by from eight to twelve bullocks in the charge of a driver and another man.

Annabella Boswell's family, with its land at Port Macquarie, was well placed to gain from the prosperity the growing wool trade had brought to New South Wales and the other infant colonies. In 1843 she notes that the 'unexampled prosperity' of the wool boom had allowed her uncle from Port Macquarie to take a house in Sydney for the winter.

> They had horses and carriages and a very large establishment, and were entertained by a very large circle of friends ... At this time they bought many beautiful things, pictures, plate, etc., and a really magnificent set of Chinese china made to order, which comprised dinner and dessert, breakfast, tea and coffee sets each complete, also hot water plates, and a set of three large and very beautiful bowls, with the Innes crest in colours on each. This china was very costly and was used only on special occasions.

A very different picture emerges from another account eventually published in London. Alexander Harris covered considerable areas of New South Wales on horseback and recorded a picture full of squalor, cruelty and misery. Near Bathurst , he recorded this scene:

> The roads excessively dusty, and all the water-holes where the bullocks usually drink dried up. Many of the poor animals we passed in teams of four, six and eight, yoked in pairs, were panting and hanging their tongues out in a manner

most painful to behold, whilst their drivers flogged, and shouted, and swore unremittingly ... The dexterity with which some of these men used the whip is quite astonishing: the report when it strikes is like a rifle's crack, and the macerated hair and flesh fly up from the spot in a little white cloud like spray.

After shearing, the roads were clogged with drays on their way to Sydney or ports groaning under the weight of wool bales. Here, the teams have paused near Nelligen in southern New South Wales.

Moruya Historical Society

The treatment of farm labour was not much better. The normal system was to employ a shepherd to look after the sheep during the day, and a hut man to tend them at night. Some station owners combined the job in one man who was expected to prevent any stock straying during any of the twenty-four hours of a day. The workers were often in a situation where they could buy the necessities of life only from their employer, and it was common practice to at least double the prices obtaining in Sydney. The farm-worker's pay was thus effectively swallowed up by the master. That applied in cases where any wages were actually paid; Harris cites examples of freemen never receiving wages. Convict shepherds were even worse off, their treatment including being flogged for misdemeanours, usually loss of stock. Often the owner lost in the end: the shepherds knew they would be flogged for one missing sheep, so once one had gone there was no incentive to control the remainder of the flock. One old shepherd whom Harris met told him that over the years he could have retrieved hundreds of his master's sheep but had not bothered because he knew he would be flogged anyway.

The reality of an employee's lot was not apparent until the hapless immigrant arrived on the run. On the surface, it seemed to the working class back in Britain that good wages were to be earned in New South Wales. In February 1835, the *Sydney Gazette* reported the publication of a booklet called *Hints Relating to Emigrants and Emigration* which reported that husbandmen were in much demand in the Australian colonies, so much so that they could earn between £10 and £12 a year with lodging and rations provided, putting them on a par with ploughmen, shepherds, shearers and other farm labourers. Fencers and field labourers were being paid between four and five shillings a week, also with lodgings and rations thrown in.

Before 1847, when the squatters were given security of tenure, the indication that any given several thousands of acres were occupied would be signified merely by the presence somewhere on that area of land of a bark humpy and a bough yard for the sheep. No other fences existed, the properties being bounded by leading ridges and embracing the valley or valleys lying between them. Because there were no fences, when a station changed hands it was usual for the purchaser to ride around the boundaries with his neighbouring settlers and thereupon agree on those boundaries; disputes would be settled by the local government commissioner. Apart from the often paralysing loneliness, the main discomforts of life were the bushrangers, destruction of stock by Aborigines and the delinquencies of assigned servants. At one point, a group of settlers was moved to write a public letter to Bourke reporting on the state of affairs.

> The interior of the colony is infested by gangs of cattle stealers and other disorderly persons ... these groups consist of freed men, who have served short sentences, or those of long sentences holding tickets-of-leave, who combine with the assigned servants to plunder the herds of their masters. Many of these men are known to possess large herds of cattle, obtained in a very short time by a series of schemes for stealing them.

Meanwhile, the blacks resented the presence of flocks and herds brought in by the squatter. They feared the firearms of the Europeans, so usually confined their attacks to unguarded sheep and cattle, although there were nevertheless numerous reports during the 1830s and 1840s of lone and unarmed shepherds being attacked and killed by groups of blacks. One account of early farm life in Victoria contains the story of a shepherd whose carelessness resulted in the loss of ninety-two sheep in one day. The owner found them 140 miles away, the Aborigines who had taken them having constructed a neat brush enclosure to contain the animals. A considerable number of sheep had already been killed and eaten, and the settler had to be content with regaining fifty of his flock. In Van Diemen's Land the situation was no better. Mrs Meredith, who left an account of her early life in early Tasmania, writes of a servant hired in 1841, a young woman who was excessively filthy in appearance, drank rum, smoked tobacco and swore. When she drank heavily it resulted in violent fits during which four men were required to hold her down.

Thomas Walker, who visited Melbourne in the mid 1830s, noted that there was a dearth of manual workers prepared to go on the land, and those who did could command wages of £40 or £50 a year with immense quantities of rations besides. Another Victorian settler at about this time found it hard to get shearers, the large station proprietors having secured all the best shearers in the district. In his first season, this man and his shepherd, with the help of a few Aborigines, washed and sheared 1,200 ewes. His own hut became the shearing shed, while the shepherd pressed the wool with a spade into a rough and primitive box made on the run. Even when settlers could find people to work for them, the master was often that in name only: the settlers were often too scared to chastise a worker for fear that — as many did — the hutkeeper or shepherd would merely run away.

Shearing itself required the squatter to lay in vast quantities of tea, sugar, tobacco, wheat and beer for the shearing teams. The shearers were paid by the score, between two and sixpence and four shillings according to the value of the wool. They provided their own shears, and were allowed two or three glasses of rum during the working day. The average shearer managed between fifty and eighty sheep a day; some were capable of clipping 120 animals, but their workmanship was usually sloppy. The boss or overseer had to be in the shed at all times lest the shearers miscount or miss the bottom wool. Each shearer vied for the sheep with the lightest and most open fleeces, a rough-coated wether being studiously avoided until it was the only one left in the pen.

Once the shearing was completed, it was essential to get the wool to Sydney as quickly as possible, owing to the fact that the prices were bound to fall toward the end of the season. The owner had to provide teams of oxen and drays which, depending on his distance from the coast, might be away for up to three months, his thoughts dwelling on them all that time. Each dray could carry between fifteen and twenty bales, a load of up to two tons, and would make between twelve and sixteen miles per day, with a halt during the noonday heat. The driver was accompanied by a 'mate' who cooked the meals and looked after the dray in the morning while the driver went to find his oxen. The return trip from the coast involved bringing back a year's supplies for the station, and this consignment would include up to seven chests of tea and a ton of sugar.

While squatting meant hardship and, worst of all, a grinding loneliness that drove some men mad, it also offered a sense of utter freedom. 'Yet so sweet was the stolen grass, that numbers of adventurous young fellows delighted in this vagrant life because it was so profitable', wrote James Bonwick as the time. Apart from the loneliness, there was the matter of diet. Bonwick reported that the inland squatter faced a breakfast consisting of a huge heap of mutton-chops, or a piece of salt beef and damper, either menu being washed down by green tea into which was stirred a great deal of sugar. This repast faced the squatter again at lunch, and yet again at supper — each and every day of the week.

Mostly, servants were poor cooks who took little trouble with the food they served gracelessly at the master's table. Thomas Walker visited one home in southern New South Wales, where he found:

> Sheep and wool are the objects chiefly thought of, they procure foreign luxuries from Sidney [sic], but prevent the production of domestic comforts in the way of eating and drinking. There is almost everywhere … a poverty of milk, butter, cheese, eggs, poultry and vegetables, to say nothing of horse-corn or hay, which are scarce, and home-brewed beer, which is rarely ever seen.

Later, visiting settlers up the Yarra River, he noted that the cottage of a settler would contain, typically, a bench, a broken cup or two , tin pannikins and a couple of knives and forks. Light was obtained by burning rags in pieces of pork fat. Being an unauthorised occupier in the early years, the squatter at first thought it not worthwhile to erect a comfortable dwelling on land from which he feared being expelled. Rolf Boldrewood, after being granted a squatting licence in Victoria during Fitzroy's administration, slept under his dray until he had time to build a cottage.

Food was difficult to keep in the Australian summer. Many settlers had come from Britain, and those who had at first lived in Van Diemen's Land before moving to the mainland had little experience of heat at its most savage. It was particularly difficult to keep meat in the summer. The animal was usually killed after sunset, the meat being cut and salted early the next morning and then placed in a cask underground.

Many squatters found kangaroo meat palatable at first, and nothing was allowed to go to waste. E.M. Gurr lost thousands of pounds on his farm during the first year and thereafter made economies by eating old ewes which had passed their breeding lives, keeping the more tasty wethers for the market. He would walk five miles to retrieve the skin from a single dead sheep. He wore his boots so long that he could put them on or take them off only by soaking them in water, so hard had they become.

Disease was a disaster when it struck a flock or herd. In the rich soil of Western Victoria footrot was a constant problem. This was usually treated by applying blues tone and butyr of antimony. Catarrh was another scourge. H. W. Haygarth in *Recollections of Bush Life in Australia* wrote:

> Life at a stock establishment, when the catarrh is raging, is a very different thing from life at ordinary times. The usual air of repose, bordering on languor, which hangs over the residence of a settler, is exchanged for a curious bustle, impatience, and feverish excitement. There is a constant succession of horsemen starting off in all directions to the various sheep stations, and returning with evidently bad news, and no better tempers. The arrival of drays loaded with unsightly carcasses, 'that do infect the air', and innumerable sheepskins hung on every fence to dry in the sun, mark the ravages of the disease; while at a distance apart, in the vicinity of water, a column of smoke points out the situation of the (tallow) boiling pans, now the last resource of the unlucky sheep-owner.

Stock from neighbouring mixed freely because there were rarely fences built to stop them, which was a severe liability if a neighbour's sheep had been hit by scab or any infectious ailment. A neighbour could be an enemy simply by neglect, and the carelessness of a shepherd could undo a year's toil to eradicate a disease.

When there was no disease or other catastrophe, the one break in the week's routine (apart from church on Sunday) was on Saturday morning when the owner would weigh out the supplies and give each man his weekly ration, typically consisting of four ounces of tea, two pounds of sugar, four ounces of tobacco, one peck of wheat and between ten and twelve pounds of beef (when it was available) although more likely it would be mutton.

The squatters soon devised methods of combating the sun and heat, one of which was to go underground much like present-day miners in parts of New South Wales and South Australia. One farmer, Alexander Harris, described the building of a 'good-sized dairy':

> To ward off excessive heat it is customary to dig out a large hole in the ground ... This hole is covered with planks, and this again still further by sheets of bark, to keep the dust or dirt from falling through on the cream; and the

whole roof is then covered over with the earth that has been dug out ... At the entrance is placed a door which is padlocked, and all round inside is ranged the keelers [shallow tubs for cooling liquids] on benches of wood or embankments of earth.

Harris found that he could easily keep the milk of forty cows by means of this arrangement. The squatters tried to lay in all their stores from Sydney or Melbourne once a year, simply because local storekeepers charged exorbitant prices, especially if they had a commodity much in demand. The up-country store was usually an ordinary slab building, containing a rude counter and shelves around the walls. It would stock slop clothing for men; hats, gown print and perfumery for women; coarse silk handkerchiefs, saddles, sheep shears, Epsom salts, tea, bacon and many other items. There were no fixed prices, prices being adjusted to the state of the market at the time. Cash was seldom exchanged, everyone using drafts drawn on accounts held with Sydney or Melbourne agents and merchants, a 'please to pay' written upon them, and passing through several hands before being presented for payment in the city.

A letter from Sydney

Meanwhile, in London, the problem of the squatters and the by now obvious inevitability of expansion of the settled areas of the colony of New South Wales was viewed by many in Whitehall in the light of the ideas of Edward Gibbon Wakefield, ideas which had been widely accepted in Britain by the mid 1830s. Wakefield was the architect of the method of colonisation in South Australia, and in the Wellington and Nelson settlements across the Tasman in New Zealand.

His theory was most effectively set out in *A Letter from Sydney*, published in 1829. Although Wakefield had never been to Australia, the letter form was a useful device. He argued the case that there was no point in giving settlers free land or land at a low price such as two shillings an acre. If the land cost nothing, then it was worth next to nothing. The settlers would not be able to sell their holdings for a reasonable price because those following them could more cheaply obtain virgin land still in the public domain.

But what concerned him more was that there should always be a plentiful supply of labour to provide the settlers with the manpower needed to develop the new colony. Convicts were of little use. The 'pure merinos' associated with Macarthur and emancipists did not agree; they were all in favour of cheap labour and cheap land, both elements being the joint bases of their wealth.

Wakefield argued that while convict labour was cheaply obtained, the convicts would probably not work hard and would almost certainly rob the settler. The other source of labour in New South Wales at the time was ex-soldiers and adventurers, neither being good material for a labouring class. Wakefield expounded the problem thus:

> Every day sees an increase in the number of employers of labour, without a proportionate increase in the number of labourers. As convicts are fairly distributed among those who want them, the general increase of demand diminishes the supply to each settler. 20,000 convicts, divided amongst 500 settlers, would give each settler forty pairs of hands ... but divide the same number of convicts amongst ten times the numbers of settlers and poverty, in respect of everything above mere subsistence, must be the lot of all. During forty years we have combined the fire and water of political economy — cheap land and cheap labour.

In 1832 Wakefield was to develop this theme. 'Transportation has furnished our new settlements with an idle and vicious population almost totally unacquainted with the business of agriculture', he wrote. In addition, the practice of granting land or making it available cheaply to those with little capital meant that the pair of hands, which might be better employed as hired help on a larger property, was engaged less productively than it might have been. Those, he argued, with sufficient capital who might otherwise have been tempted to settle in Australia were deterred from doing so by the prospect of cultivating the land with their own hands; even if they were prepared to do so, much of the better land had already been parcelled our to persons unable to cultivate it properly. Wakefield's answer was that those people with capital should be offered land at a price they could afford, but that the price should be greater than poorer settlers could manage, thus consigning the latter to become a substantial pool of available labour.

The government takes on the squatters

While this discussion went on in London, in Sydney Governor Bourke was faced with the instruction to restrain the limits of settlement but without the means of being able to do so. His only answer had been the annual licence, together with commissioners to enforce its conditions, but these men had little real power. It was not until Governor Gipps provided the commissioners with mounted police that they were able to control the chaos, chicanery and even murder which were part and parcel of the early squatting expansion. By the middle of 1840, 673 runs had been licensed, and these licensed settlers had no intention of allowing themselves, their million sheep and 300,000 cattle to be driven off the land. Gradually houses and fences appeared on the Australian landscape.

In 1847 new regulations were promulgated. Gipps was coming to terms with the inevitable; he knew by this time that the system of annual licences was not going to work. He was also aware that the demands for self-government were growing. The Orders-in-Council were approved and proclaimed at a time when the settlers had already passed Moreton Bay on their way up to Queensland in the north, and in the south had penetrated the eastern region of Victoria (later to be known as Gippsland). It was already seven years since transportation to New South Wales had been abolished, and the colony was now a society of free men which looked to the future. Gipps's power was informally and formally limited by the growing role of the Legislative Council, clearly dominated by squatter interests. His view was that some land should be saved for the future, that all the grazing land occupied by the squatters should not be alienated forever. The squatters, of course, took precisely the contrary view. The 1847 regulations, which formulated the system of dividing land into settled, unsettled and intermediate, were made possible only by the power and influence of the squatter lobby. The regulations consolidated the squattocracy's position as the chief collective power in New South Wales. The governor now conceded the right of these men to remain on the land they had acquired by all manner of irregular means (see Appendix for names and details). Several of the large land holders controlled several runs (Ben Boyd ended up paying an £80 quit-rent on 388,000 acres). The squatters were supported by the merchants and traders of the cities, whose best customers they were. This combined power served to thwart Gipps, who was basically an anti-squatting governor. These men had begun to look upon their runs as their own long before the 1847 regulations confirmed their occupancy. It should be said, though, that their clamour for security of tenure was understandable — they had thousands of animals and an established way of life. The new law fixed tenure at fourteen years, but the squatters knew that the governor had conceded the right of pre-emption of the land. The squatters had gained all that they asked for, and got far more than they could ever have realistically hoped to get a few years earlier.

A record load of 150 bales weighing almost 18 tons.

National Library of Australia

Fences went up, stock disease was attacked more resolutely, and commodious woolsheds began to dot the countryside. The squatters could marry now that they had built decent houses and they began to enjoy the fruits of their labour, filling their new homes with furniture and books. Squatters began to spend more time in town and, in Melbourne particularly, they were set apart from the rest of the population by the smart clothes and expensive boots they wore while in town. When the Melbourne Club was founded, the majority of its first members were squatters from up country. The social season to some extent revolved around the times of the years the landholders were able to visit town, and they were favoured guests at balls, dinners and race meetings. At home in the country the women brought with them good cooking and church going.

But while the squatters were satisfied, the growing colonial public in the towns was not. The land was locked up, and this fact produced bitter jealousy against the favoured few for many years to come.

Chapter 3

On Our Selection

Storing the harvester after the crop has been brought in.

National Library of Australia

FOR THE MOMENT, the squatters could take stock of their situation. They had land and, by the late 1840s, they could feel that it might or would be theirs forever. After all, did they not have the political power, especially in the Legislative Council of New South Wales, to ensure that the state of affairs continued? There lay over the anarchy of the great land-grab the palimpsest of legalised tenure.

But new pressures were beginning to arise. There entered the Australian colonies more free migrants with dreams of owning land and securing what could never be theirs at home, a farm of their own. These people were actually prepared to buy the land, and the governments badly needed the money the migrants were prepared to pay. The pressure to 'unlock the land' was growing apace. In 1846 the Chartist movement had reached its zenith in England. The movement, whose people's charter demanded, among other things, possession of the land, drew tens of thousands to its meetings. So the immigrants had a model, and upon that they founded land leagues in Victoria and New South Wales. A Land Convention met in Melbourne in 1857 and demanded the end of squatters' rights and, in its place, selection of land at fixed prices. The land-hungry of Australia were also strongly influenced by the parallel pressures which had grown in the United States, which led there to the Homestead Act of 1862. The land question was resolving into a struggle of the original squatters, wrote one contemporary observer, 'and their heirs, executors and assigns, against the inroad of a hungry herd of selectors'.

The pressure for land was felt particularly in Victoria. This latest Australasian colony had experienced a phenomenal increase in its population, from 77000 in 1851 to just over half a million ten years later. By 1861, 35,000 men were employed on farms in Victoria and the area under cropping had passed 400,000 acres. The reason for much of this activity was the discovery of gold, and development of land had been particularly rapid in the areas surrounding the goldfields. Farmers found the miners to be a good ready local market for their produce. Land near Ballarat was soon fetching £5 an acre. Later on, as the Victorian government embarked upon a policy of having no farmer farther than a half day's ride from a railway station, pressures for close settlement were to grow in other parts of the colony. But, for the moment, the primitive communications of the time — the carts bogging down in the mud, the weeks or months spent on the road to deliver the wool clip and return with a year's supplies, the threat of bushrangers to the lone traveller, the simple waste of manhours spent on the road rather than the farm-meant that outside the goldfields there was not the same prosperity. There was, too, the factor that many of the men who took up land had little capital or were often indolent or ignorant of good farm practice. Ignorance of the principles of agriculture is a factor which appears to have plagued Australian farming in its first hundred years. The attitude that land should be cropped intensively for as long as it could bear a payable crop and then be abandoned for another virgin block was as prevalent in Victoria in the 1850s as it had been at Liberty Plains in the 1790s.

The ideal was, alas, far different from the reality. A book, *How to Settle in Victoria*, published in London, counselled the new settler that to take up land in the colony he should begin with a frame tent, three to six months' stores and warm clothing. He was to take on two good grubbers and splitters to clear the land, and he would need to pay £1 for each tree grubbed from his land. Other men should be engaged to fence the land, three-rail fences with gum posts being advised. With the initial five acres thus cleared, it should be apportioned:

1½ acres	Potatoes
1 acre	Turnips
¼ acre	Peas and beans
¾ acre	Cabbages, broccoli
¼ acre	Onions
¼ acre	Carrots and parsnips
¾ acre	Flower garden, herb beds, nursery
¼ acre	Yards and paths.

As more land was cleared, five acres should be sown in fodder for horses, four acres in oaten hay and one in lucerne.

This Arcadian prospect was somewhat different from reality. In 1860 the Victorian Parliament passed the Nicholson Act whose original concept had been to provide some form of system to the sale of land. But it was so amended by squatter interests during its parliamentary passage that it ended up enabling squatters to buy more land. Nevertheless, the forces of land justice could not be denied for much longer. New legislation was soon proposed and passed. In 1862 it became possible for anyone in New South Wales to buy between forty and 320 acres of Crown land, while the same year saw Victoria provide for blocks of from forty to 640 acres, in both colonies the price being £1 an acre. There were conditions regarding improvements and fences, with part of the purchase money being used to pay the passages of new immigrants. By 1868 Queensland had provided for selection, and the following year South Australia followed suit.

In New South Wales and Victoria, where selection was pioneered, the problem with the legislation was that there were too many loopholes through which the squatters could, so to speak, drive a bullock dray in order to retain control of 'their' land.

They employed various means of acquiring more land, among the more notorious being 'dummying'. The squatter arranged for someone else, either a relative or someone paid for the role, to select a block, the idea being that after a few years it would be quietly transferred to the ownership of the squatter. Sometimes the 'dummy' would renege on the deal, and there was little the squatter could do. Another system was 'gridironing', where the squatter bought the land round a waterhole or along either side of the creek. The rest of the land was useless without access to the water, so the squatter retained de facto use of it, for nothing. Then there were the 'flying huts' — movable buildings which could be dismantled and taken from one selection to the other. The Government insisted on improvements to the land, and the 'flying hut' could be transferred from one block to another just ahead of the inspector.

Debt, drudgery and despair

The failure of the selection legislation to work properly meant that much of the best land, more suited to cropping, was retained for pastoralism by the squatter. It seems likely that, of the 20 million acres of New South Wales alienated by 1883, much was used to hold back settlement. Those settlers who yearned to farm the land had to bypass the rich central districts of New South Wales, the flatlands of the Darling Downs or the rolling pastures of the western districts of Victoria and head, instead, for the far less attractive prospects of the mallee. A forty or even 320 acre block might suit anyone who wanted to farm in England or Ireland, but such minuscule selections were frequently impractical in Australian conditions. For most of the small settlers, selection came to mean a life spent in poverty, misery and abject loneliness. The key was to live thriftily, growing your own vegetables, killing your own mutton or beef and grinding your own corn. A man would have to find as much outside work as possible and would work for much of the year as a carrier, shearer, timber-getter, kangaroo shooter, runner of wild horses or fencing contractor. The woman and children would be left to keep the selection going, with the children inevitably having little or no time for going to school.

Squalor was the norm. One of its products, Arthur Davis, was to immortalise the life of the selector under the pseudonym of Steele Rudd. He portrayed the life with a rough humour which Australia needed. The author of *On Our Selection* exaggerated both the action and the situation, and produced larger-than-life absurdities, but he knew what he was talking about. The first house built on his father's selection had one room and the floor was a mixture of sand and fresh cow-dung, renewed each month. The doors were kept closed with timber pegs and the slab walls were so fashioned that it was possible to survey the surrounding area through the cracks.

Most selectors never made it. For example, in one area near Toowoomba in Queensland a block containing 156 selections, each of eighty acres, was taken up between 1876 and 1881. By 1903, only fifty-two of the original families were still in possession. The story was repeated everywhere else.

The selectors lived in bark humpies. The children were driving horse teams by the time they were seven while the women were slaves to keeping their husbands and families fed and clothed. Nothing was wasted. The men would often disappear to a nearby tavern and drink themselves into oblivion, but for the women there were no such escapes. Many went mad.

Early farming was a family affair, although the clothes on the boys suggest that this day they were not out toiling in the fields. But the woman of the house would have brought tea and food out for smokos and lunchtimes. The 1904 harvest at Rose Dale Farm near Cuballing, north of Narrogin in Western Australia, has clearly been interrupted for everyone to pose for the camera.

Western Australian Newspapers

What little gains the selectors made were eaten away by debt. Under the terms of selection, their purchase of the land required improvements, and this meant borrowing money or running up debts with the local storekeeper. The interest rates could be as high as 35 per cent. In *On Our Selection* the father sells his entire corn crop to the local shopkeeper in order to pay off his account, only to find that still leaves £3 in debt outstanding. He goes home and stares into the fire and, when his wife sees the account, she, too, is stunned into silence. While many crumpled under the weight of debt, drudgery and despair, others clung on by means of contract work as a rouseabout or fencer or by resorting to stealing stock.

Few farmers cared about turning their efforts into producing the comforts of life. Even by the turn of the century, a visitor to a sugar plantation in northern New South Wales remarked upon how nothing but cane was grown-right up to the house, in fact. When the visitor suggested to the farmer and his wife that it might be profitable to vary their cropping and, say, plant an acre of pineapples, it was greeted with outrage. 'Pineapples!' said the wife. 'Pineapples! Do you think we'd grow a mean crop like that. No, we ain't going to grow no pines on this farm.' The writer noted that wherever he went the object seemed to be the raising of as big a crop as possible of the one kind, whether it was wheat, sugar cane or fruit, or concentrating on one type of livestock farming. The wheatgrower thought of nothing but wheat:

> He scratches, or indifferently ploughs his land or prepares it in some way or other, or, maybe, depends on the self-sown seed, without any preparation whatever. Sometimes an attempt is made to raise a crop amongst quite newly ringbarked timber, and frequently, crops are raised for years between innumerable stumps. Such a rough system of farming may be excusable and all very well for a start: but, unfortunately, the same kind of practice continues, year after year, on the same farms, and no attention is ever given to the desirability for improvement, or the importance of raising as much as possible from the farm for family requirements.

One farmer who arrived in Queensland showed that it was possible to work hard and acquire land. Writing anonymously twenty-four years later, he described how he had come to the new colony in 1864 and hired himself out as a farm hand for £45 a year. Of that he saved £40 with which he bought himself a quarter-acre allotment at Ipswich. He then worked for two more years for £75 with rations and board, and was able at the end to buy two further allotments for a total of £70. Then, besides working these allotments, he worked as a contractor, which enabled him to buy an area of twenty-two acres for £66, with a further £66 having to be spent on fencing. By the time the Queensland selection laws came into force, the man was in a position to select a further 120 acres. No wonder he avowed that he had never regretted coming to Queensland.

Apart from the pressures of debt and privation, the selector faced a mammoth task to make his land productive. The early spread of the pasroralist had not been hampered too much by the need to clear ground. They first sought out land that was already partially clear with native grasses. The stock was allowed to wander freely, only being rounded up at night by the hutkeeper.

Clearing the land for crops

Crops were a different matter altogether. Farmers had to clear the land, which was often a long, arduous and time-consuming business. An account in the *New South Wales Agricultural Gazette*, published last century for intending new settlers, outlined the recommended process for clearing the land. The usual and best method, it told the settler, was to ringbark the timber ten years previous to clearing, a process which tended to 'aerate and sweeten the soil, thereby increasing its productiveness.' The cost of clearing one acre of live timber was about the same as for five or six acres of dead timber; the dead trees burned easily and their roots were more swiftly extracted from the ground. To clear green timber, the settler was advised to possess the following tackle:

A two-inch best steel wire rope, from ninety to 100 feet in length, with a swivel, three links, and a hook attached on each end of the rope, made very stout and strong, to be able to bear a good strain.

A close-linked stout chain of suitable length for a sling, provided with a strong ring in each end-link; one ring should be small enough to pass through the other. A straight barrel of a tree, about equal to the drawing power of two pairs of bullocks, provided with strong chains around the butt ends, one to hook to the bullock team, and the other to hook on to the wire rope, which is in turn hooked with the sling placed around the standing tree.

A light, strong ladder of about twenty feet, to carry the sling up to the required height, completes the outfit.

To provide the motive power for all this equipment, the farmer needed a team of six to eight pairs of bullocks — that is, up to sixteen beasts — and they could usually manage to pull down a tree of between 24 and 30 inches diameter in the first pull.

The settler intending to grow crops did not have the time or energy to get rid of all the trees at once. He would normally begin by taking out the larger trees and ring barking the remainder, with the crop planted in the areas which were cleared between the trunks. Year by year, the trees would be gradually removed.

In the scrublands, the approach was to knock over the native vegetation by use of large rollers pulled by bullocks. When the farmers came to tackle the mallee country in South Australia and Victoria the land had to be cleared by axe. One mallee farmer wrote an article some years later in the *Journal of Agriculture and Industry of South Australia* describing his method of clearing mallee scrub. For grubbing, he got a good sound stringybark lever, 27 feet long and about one foot in diameter at the thick end. If there was any knack in grubbing, it was in the starting of the stump. Instead of pulling the stump right out at first, the settler would start half a dozen and then trail them all out together.

Once the stumps were out, the land had to be worked. In the days before manufactured ploughs, the preliminary to planting wheat was to make a plough. First, the settler selected a piece of wood for a beam, then two others for the handles. The foot was then formed by splitting part of the trunk, the woodwork being completed by a length of red gum serving as a mould board. All that was needed after that were a few bolts and an iron share from the local blacksmith. The farmer could turn over about four acres a week with this piece of equipment, provided he had enough bullocks. The problem with this type of implement was that it broke when it hit a tree stump. There was also a similarly primitive harrow which failed to break all the large clods of earth, the job having to be completed with a mallet. The crop was harvested with sickle or hook, and hiring reapers to help usually involved a wage of a pound an acre plus keep and two glasses of rum a day. After threshing, winnowing was carried out by the time-tested if somewhat clumsy method of throwing a shovelful of grain at a time into the wind.

The first major breakthrough was the stump-jump plough, invented in 1876 by Robert Bowyer Smith in Adelaide. It was a revolutionary idea: the plough, when it hit a stump, would ride over the top of it instead of breaking. It transformed the economics of land development, much land having been forfeited by selectors because they had been crushed by the cost of clearing it. For example, in South Australia in the 1870s, the cost of clearing and grubbing land could be anywhere between £2 and £7 an acre, even the lowest cost being a substantial, if not exorbitant, sum at the time. The impact of the stump-jump plough was to make it possible for settlers to clear quickly and cultivate marginal land in low-rainfall areas. The plough was refined and improved as time went on, but its original concept — that a weighted and hinged body could be designed to fall back into a furrow after riding over the stump, and not break as the more primitive ploughs had done — was the breakthrough. It allowed Australian settlers to contemplate cultivating land which, because of the cost of total clearance and grubbing, would have been previously considered suitable only for sheep and cattle to graze.

That was one problem solved. Farmers also needed some form of mechanised harvesting. This was especially so in South Australia and Western Australia where labour was short; and in South Australia the problem was exacerbated by the speed at which new wheat areas were being developed. In

1843 Governor George Grey had to send 150 soldiers out into the fields to help in harvesting the crop, but that was a stopgap measure. In the previous year it had been recognised that the shortage of manual labour (in Wakefield's model colony, too) for harvesting the wheat crops of South Australia was so serious that agricultural development would have come to a standstill had not some mechanical means been found. Such was the need for innovation that a prize of £40 was offered by an Adelaide newspaper for a successful design.

Of the sixteen entries, none was successful in being good enough to merit the prize. Most were straight cutting machines in various forms, but one introduced a new idea — a 'comb and beaters' mechanism which gathered the grain without either cutting or reaping the plant. It was dismissed by the judges, and its inventor John Wrathall Bull was to be a disappointed man, for one of those who came to see all the entries was John Ridley.

Ridley was not a competitor; although he was working on a cutting machine, it was not completed in time to enter the newspaper competition. What he did was return home with Bull's idea clearly imprinted on his mind. Bull conceived the idea; Ridley was to make it work. Three months after the newspaper competition had been held Ridley had a working model of his stripper. *The Adelaide Observer* reported in November 1843 that the machine would 'collect the ears, thresh them out, winnow the corn and fill the bags'. *The South Australian* described the machine thus:

> It has a number of spikes in front to collect the ears, which, by the forward motion, are brought under the influence of the drum. The drum takes off the ears, or rather beats the grain out of them in the usual manner and the process so far is completed.

Bull pressed his claim over the next few years, writing to newspapers in Adelaide pointing out that Ridley's invention was built on a concept of his. He was soon joined by others who bore witness to the fact that in September 1843 Bull had entered a 'comb and beaters' stripper for the competition. Ridley never acknowledged the debt, and his daughter published a book in 1902 disputing Bull's claims. But there were early doubts. In March 1845 *The South Australian* conceded in an editorial that Bull 'may have' invented the method. Then in 1882 the South Australian Government made Bull an award of £250 for his contribution to agricultural machinery. Nevertheless, the stripper had been born.

The invention meant that the colony could expand its wheat production in the knowledge that whatever was grown could be harvested. The effect of mechanical reapers and threshers was demonstrated on the Inveralochy Estate, near Goulburn in New South Wales, where the owner, a Mr Craig, had bought the machine after seeing it in South Australia. That was in 1848. According to an account in the *Goulburn Evening Penny Post* written many years later, a man who had seen the machine in action described it as drawn by eight bullocks. When it was in motion it apparently made a noise resembling escaping steam. It stopped only when it was necessary to empty the threshed grain onto a tarpaulin, at which time a little oil was applied to its moving parts. The straw, which was left standing the full length of the stalk, was later burnt. It was possible to harvest 21 acres in three and a half days with this machine.

Wheat becomes a viable proposition

James Ruse was the first farmer in Australia to produce wheat on a commercial basis, but it was the New South Wales Officer Corps which developed major plantings in the early years. The civilian men of the land were too interested in sheep.

Between 1825 and 1855, largely owing to the 'put everything on four feet' philosophy, wheat cultivation in both New South Wales and Van Diemen's Land failed to expand in line with population growth. The main problem was that transport was in short supply, and was expensive because of the time involved. Again, wheat was not as profitable as wool and meat in the boom years, and before the days of mechanisation there simply was not the labour to plant and harvest the crops. It was not until the railway came that wheat became an attractive and viable proposition.

A similar shortage of wheat plagued the new colony on the Swan River in Western Australia. In 1831 it was noted that of the 1 million acres alienated, a mere 200 were under cultivation, of which 160 were producing wheat. The British Government had wanted to avoid expense and responsibility in the establishment of a colony on the Swan, so that land was granted regardless of the applicant's ability to make improvements. Like New South Wales and Van Diemen's Land in their early years, Western Australia relied in those first years on imported wheat, and the failure by some ships to arrive brought the new colony close to famine.

The Swan settlement had been founded in 1829, and a year later 1500 people had settled on the site of the present city of Perth. Migrants got forty acres for every £3 they invested, and the amount of land granted was blatantly optimistic if not profligate. When the capital needed for land included either money, livestock equipment or a settler's pension, it induced many of the immigrants to overreach themselves.

Their pioneering optimism was quickly blunted when they realised what confronted them on the Swan. They found that the coastal soils were poor in quality, and later discovered that much of the interior of Western Australia was too low in phosphates to support wheat. Some of them had been given far more land than they could manage, having spent money on additional land acquisition which would have been more wisely invested in improvements.

Progress was slow. By 1835, the directors of the Agricultural Society of Western Australia were able to report that the colony possessed 84 horses, 78 mares, 307 cows, 96 working cattle, 97 bulls and steers, 3545 sheep, 492 goats and 374 pigs. At that time, the elephantine slowness with which land was being brought into production was revealed: only 564 acres were planted in wheat, 100 in barley, 116 in oats, 29 in kaffir corn and maize, 15 in potatoes, 94 in other crops, half an acre in vines, while 118 acres lay fallow, this last being due to the shortage of seed. The society was, however, proud of its having five British breeds of cattle: Devon, Yorkshire, Durham, Alderney and Ayrshire. The report noted that the farmers of Western Australia were keen to replace their large-tailed sheep with merinos.

The first wool had been exported to London in 1832 but, being dirty and badly packed, it fetched a very poor price. However, by 1835 there had been a clip of 5884 pounds and much greater care had been taken with the cleaning and packing of the wool.

In the 1840s the agricultural production in Western Australia was beginning to make considerable leaps forward. In 1838 the Swan colony produced 22,000 bushels of wheat; in 1843 there was again another good wheat crop, and grape and fruit growing were established; in 1848 barley, oats, rye, maize and potatoes were all being produced in noticeable quantities; and the Avon Valley was settled. But the depression which had hit all the colonies in this period lowered the prices received on the home markets, and in 1849 Western Australia received only £20,000 in export payments.

There was no question that, twenty years after its foundation, the new colony was struggling. By 1850 the population was only 6000, and hired labour was acutely short. The desperate settlers had no alternative but to request London to declare Western Australia a convict settlement, ten years after New South Wales had seen the last convict arrive, and only three years before Van Diemen's Land abandoned the system. In 1850 the first shipload arrived, and these were followed over the next eighteen years by another 9000 men. The convicts provided both the labour and the market upon which the wheat and wool industries could develop. Many of the convicts were given tickets-of-leave soon after they set foot in the Swan colony so that they could find employment with settlers. They gave the economy of the colony the fillip it needed, but the time of penal colonies had passed; both in Britain and the eastern Australian colonies there was opposition to continued transportation and in 1867 it was abandoned.

One of the most indignant opponents of transportation to the Swan was the government of South Australia, which had been founded by free settlers in the spirit and temper of English liberalism. It was more a colony in the Wakefield mould. The repeal of the British Corn Laws in 1846 had made it possible for South Australians to send wheat back to the old country. By 1850 more than 40,000 acres of South Australia were planted in wheat, and the discovery of gold in Victoria provided a new and large market across the border. The rise in prices of up to £ 1 per bushel and the development of mechanised threshing had made feasible the spread into more marginal farming areas.

"Farm life 1890-1900" is the description with this photograph. The location is not known, but it would be representative of smallholder farming in Australia, the growing crops the dream of the selector.

John Oxley Library

Like the settlers in inland New South Wales who found that 320 acres were too few with which to make a decent living, so too did the wheat growers who had gone inland from Adelaide or Port Pirie find that the allocated 80-acre block was just not enough to provide a living for themselves and their families. The invention of the stripper allowed farmers to contemplate managing much larger properties, while the growing railway network moving upward from Adelaide made it possible to extend the colony's frontiers. There was the added appeal that wheat, unlike 'everything on four feet', did not require expensive fencing.

The northward movement of settlers could, it seemed at the time, know no bounds, even though in 1865 the Surveyor-General of South Australia, G. W. Goyder, drew his now historic line upon the map as a limit for northward expansion and settlement beyond which no farmer should venture other than at his peril. The line, which neatly bisected South Australia, was Goyder's guide to which areas had insufficient rainfall to sustain cropping. Of course, he was eventually proved right but at the time the settlers were nor interested in listening to the warning. The newspapers of South Australia waged a narrow campaign against Goyder. At first, it seemed as though the Surveyor-General might have been wrong; the early 1870s were years of plentiful rain, and wheat sprang from the ground.

Alas, the bounty was shortlived. In the 1880s the inevitable dry years arrived. The Goyder line had been, as a result of the outcry, wiped from the map in 1874. Although one can now see quite clearly how perceptive Goyder had been, the carchcry in 1874 had been, 'Go north, young man'. The possibilities seemed boundless — until the drought arrived.

The years 1881 and 1892 were ones of severe drought, and were followed by another ten dry years. More than half a million acres were abandoned. Meanwhile, much good grazing land in inland South Australia had been ruined by the plough. In fact, much of the opposition to Goyder's line had been based on the suspicion that the Surveyor-General was playing into the hands of the pasroralists who were then trying to block the northward expansion of agriculture. One letter which had appeared in an Adelaide newspaper in 1874, the year his line was abolished, summed up the ridicule heaped on Goyder's head:

> I came into a store at Pekina, on the other side of the 'rainfall' [line], on Tuesday, May 4, at about nine o'clock in the forenoon, wet to the skin, and it rained steady all that day and night and part of the next day, and I defy Mr Goyder or any other man to say at which side of the hedge most rain fell.

The other problems the South Australian farmers encountered were weeds, stinking smut and red rust. Farmers were often forced to begin sowing before the weeds had germinated, giving the weeds a head start on the crop. Stinking smut, or bunt as it was more correctly called, was detectable when the crop became bluish in colour. The grains were filled with a black powder inside the husk, the powder being the spores of the fungus. When the grain passed through the reaper or thresher the black powder was mixed with the rest of the grain and the greater part of a crop was thus infected. Red rust was a particularly nasty problem in Western Australia. In 1873 it affected 6000 acres of muchneeded wheat crops.

The real pest was the rabbit

It seems that rabbits in Australia arrived with the First Fleet, and it was common for the early settlers to keep white rabbits. There are references to them also in the early history of the Port Phillip Bay settlement. In the 1850s and 1860s landowners released rabbits in order to provide a source of game. At Castlemaine in Victoria in the early 1860s some settlers tried to farm rabbits in order to provide some relief from the diet of mutton and beef.

In their native England, the rabbits had a defined place in the ecology of the countryside. They were kept in their place by the nature of close settlement and the consequent heavy competition for space and food. In Australia, there was no such great competition, especially after the rabbits had increased to such numbers that the native cats, eagles and hawks could no longer be a threat to their continued existence. The country was sparsely populated and there was plenty of natural cover. By 1880 the first legislation was being passed in an attempt to combat the spread of rabbits. Fences were built to stop them, one being from Swan Hill to Lake Albacutya and then on to the South Australian border, with boundary riders employed to keep the fence in good repair.

The rabbits, of course, got through, even when Western Australia built rabbit-proof fences over great swathes of territory. For example, the Number Three Fence ran from the Indian Ocean coast north of Geraldton hundreds of miles eastwards to a junction south of Paroo where it met Number One Rabbit Proof Fence, which extended from the north of the state right to the south coast near Hopetoun, In 1887 the Victorian and South Australian Governments erected a rabbit fence between the two colonies from the south coast to the Murray River — 290 miles in all. Apart from boundary riders, men had to be taken on at each gate to make sure that it was not left open by people passing through. But the system broke down when landowners typically made little effort to keep the rabbit fence repaired when it was on their property. Furthermore, the gates were frequently left open, and sandhills built up at several places along the fence providing a convenient land bridge for the rabbits. So the rabbits moved into South Australia and beyond the Murray.

In 1903 Daisy Bates left an account of a visit to a station eleven years earlier when she had taken part in a rabbit drive. After arriving by train at Hay in New South Wales, she took a Cobb and Co. coach toward the Lachlan River. It was the rainy season and the roads, mere bush tracks at the best of times, now looked more like rivers of mud. Out of the window of the coach she could see that 'the rabbits were there in myriads gambolling round the salt bush tufts that seemed to be the sole herbiage on these plains, and they were manifestly so perfectly at home that they merely cocked their ears at us when we passed, and continued their gambols'. The dogs, she wrote, did not chase rabbits because for everyone that they began to pursue, fifty more would start running around; the dogs contented themselves with killing any rabbit that ran in front of them. Her host employed men to kill the rabbits (by snaring, poisoning and shooting) but the other selectors nearby made no such efforts, making this man's measures rather pointless.

Came the morning of the drive, and many of the squatters and those of the selectors who wanted to make the effort, drawn from a distance of ninety miles and accompanied by about 200 dogs, lined up to drive bunny to his doom. First, about three-quarters of an acre was hemmed in by wire netting, leaving a twenty-foot opening at one end for the rabbits to enter. Then the men and women were to ride quietly into the bush for about eight or nine miles, and then they were to turn their horses toward the enclosure and form, as nearly as possible, a semicircle. They were to ride back slowly toward the pen, each person being required to 'yell, shriek, scream, and make all the outcry of which our lungs were capable'.

It was impossible for the rabbits to slip through because of the string of dogs running in front of the line of horses. Daisy Bates continued:

> As we warmed up to our work and the 'don't care' feeling set in, and we had become less ashamed (the women of our party) of giving out hideous noises, it became a' matter of competition with us as to who should 'take the cake' in that contest. We screeched, we yelled, we laughed, we cackled, we crowed, we (those of us who had heard it) set forth the Aboriginal warcry.

She was astounded by the varieties of rabbits which were shuffled thus to their doom: from coal black to piebald to brown, grey and white.

Most of these rabbits were successfully herded into the enclosure, the few which attempted escape being hastily despatched by the dogs. The men then proceeded to slaughter the captives. The count for the day's work was about 4000, with possibly another 1000 killed by the dogs.

But even a casual visitor, such as Daisy Bates, could see that this was no solution.

> Early next morning a trench was dug, and the rabbits were shovelled into it; and when we rode over the same ground in the afternoon it did not seem to me that we had made any perceptible difference in the number of the rabbits; they appeared just as numerous as ever.

New South Wales tried the bounty system. In 1887 the government paid a bounty on 2,7000,000 scalps. In 1890 a rabbit fence was built along the western boundary of the colony. That same year the Queensland Government built a fence of 648 miles along the New South Wales border, and the gates were strictly patrolled. The rabbits merely paused, and soon were pouring north to the extremes of Queensland. Local fences intended to protect uninfested areas were similarly ineffectual.

Respite came only in times of drought, when the fences did actually manage to contain millions of rabbits trying to move to other regions to escape the dry. It was a common sight at these times to see thousands of dead rabbits along one side of a fence, having perished in a vain attempt to get beyond it. During a drought, the farmers put out poisoned water, which successfully killed thousands of them, so that by the end of the great drought in 1903 the areas which had been most severely affected by the lack of rain were largely clear of rabbits.

In 1888, New South Wales set up a commission of inquiry into the rabbit problem. It was this inquiry which resulted in trapping being abandoned. Evidence before the commission made it clear that trappers shifted as soon as rabbits became scarce in any particular area, and while they were away the population recovered. One station manager told the inquiry that he could put strychnine on peaches and kill 500 rabbits in two days. The inquiry was told that Menindie station had 107 rabbiters, each man with between fifteen and twenty traps; in December 1887 they had delivered 106,282 skins. The station spokesman said that, despite that kill, he believed that the trappers were having little effect on the rabbit population of Menindie station.

The manager of Langawarra station said that he employed up to sixty trappers, that he had had them in one camp for four months, and when they left there seemed to be just as many rabbits as ever. On Taraweynia station there were 161 men employed exclusively to trap the pest and they killed half a million rabbits. The superintending inspector of the Rabbit Department said that the killing of half a million rabbits seemed to make no impression on the population, and in fact the rabbiters drove the animals on to land that was previously clear of them. The rabbit inspector at Wilcannia stated that there were more rabbits around after the trappers had been there than there were before the men arrived.

There were no easy answers to the rabbit problem, nor to several other major headaches now confronting the Australian farmer.

Chapter 4
A Cheerless Life

On the Wallaby Track – a term used to describe the life of itinerant workers and swagmen and then the title of the famous painting of 1896 by Frederick McCubbin – applies to the men shown here. A team of shearers that have 'cut out' at one station now move on to the next job.

National Library of Australia

RAILWAYS TRANSFORMED THE farming of Australia. Until the steel road starting pressing out into the vast hinterland, distance was the enemy — it devoured time and energy, and was sometimes fraught with danger, natural or man-made. Once the Australian colonies developed a taste for railways, however, there was no holding them. In 1875 there were 1,600 miles of tracks; in 1891, 9,998 miles, in 1921, 23,229 miles. Victoria pioneered, and New South Wales followed, the principle of having no farmer farther than half a day's journey from the nearest railway station. Each town and settlement lobbied furiously for the lines to pass there — a railway station became the true mark of progress — and when the lines were laid it was the occasion for triumphant celebrations. The arrival of a survey team was greeted with joy; after them came the railway workers whose job it was to form and lay the track and they, too,we welcomed at each town. In the enthusiasm of the age, lines were even built where there was no need for them. When a line was built across the Murray from Robinvale toward Lette , a remote spot in New South Wales, on the basis that the line would encourage wheat-growing, it managed between 1929 and 1935 to justify on average one train a year. The onset of the depression meant that the tracks were never built as far as Lette , and in 1935 the track that had been laid was abandoned. Another track in the Mallee, opened in 1929, was unused for the first year because there was not enough traffic available for a train to be run along it. In South Australia the disregard of the Goyder line and the consequent northward push of settlers encouraged the railway builders to follow them, so that lines such as that to Quorn and onward to Oodnadatta were soon under way.

The most extraordinary examples of the farmers demanding, and getting, railways were in the Riverina and Western Australia. The Riverina was the battleground for the Victorian and New South Wales governments. The former controlled much of the region's economic life by having built a railway from Melbourne to Echuca, to capture the traffic from the river boats. Even by 1889 the river traffic was still extremely active, there being 82 steamers and 59 barges operating on the river system, most of the cargo coming from New South Wales and being shipped through Victoria. The New South Wales authorities were determined to retaliate, and one of the measures was the line built to Bourke at the northern end of the Darling River, so as to corner the wool traffic which had been going down river to Echuca. The Victorians then extended their railway across the Murray and on to Deniliquin in New South Wales. In the year ending June 1890 this line carried 336,000 sheep, 333 head of cattle, 585 tons of wool and 58,817 bushels of wheat, all taken south to Melbourne. Over the last years of the century, the government in Sydney authorised a whole network of railways through the Riverina, some of them still open today to serve the annual wheat harvest — but, alas, many are not, the legacy of the fading of the railway age in Australia.

A graphic illustration of the effect of the railways on agricultural production was given to a Victorian Royal Commission in 1883. Before the railway reached the western Victorian town of Horsham, farmers there had paid four shillings a bag for wheat carried to the railhead at Stawell. When the line reached Horsham that heavy impost was eliminated, replaced by a minimal increase in railing costs. As railways spread into the countryside settlers put more land under wheat, knowing they had a means by which to transport the harvest. In the Riverina in the 1889-90 season, 120,000 bushels of wheat were stored in farms owing to lack of transport to the markets. The cost of carting by dray to a station could be borne (albeit with difficulty) in good years, but in those seasons when the price of wheat fell to as low as two shillings and sixpence a bushel, the money received would partly disappear in transport charges. Carriage to the station could cost sixpence a bushel, on top of which was the rail freight. In bad years, many a farmer would revert to grazing rather than produce wheat for minimal reward.

In Western Australia the proliferation of lines was staggering. A Royal Commission on immigration in 1905 had recommended that a farmer should not have to cart produce by road more than fifteen miles. If the state was to secure the fullest development of its agricultural resources "all considerable areas of agricultural land must have a fifteen mile rail service". Initial rail development in Western Australia had been dictated by mining discoveries, but from 1906 lines were pushed out from already established main railway routes. Between 1906 and 1931, 2,093 miles of agricultural lines were laid.

Lines — eventually — went almost everywhere; perhaps we should say anywhere, such was the profligacy of construction. As I have written elsewhere,

> Picture a small wayside country station. It is unmanned, but there is a siding with a few empty four-wheeler wagons. These wagons were either emptied of bagged fertiliser by the local farmer to whom they were consigned or perhaps dropped off to allow that farmer to load baled wool or bagged wheat. On the platform sit cream cans — full, as it happens — so there must be a train due to collect them and transport the contents to the nearest butter factory. Until that train arrives, there will be hardly a sound apart from the wind in the trees behind the station. Eventually the train comes, the cream cans are collected and, within a minute of the train's departure, the place is once more silent. It could have been anywhere of hundreds of places in Australia, fifty to one hundred years ago.

> — *Ghost Railways of Australia*
> by Robin Bromby, 2006

Water, water — but not everywhere

The other revolutionary technological innovation was irrigation. The then Victorian Minister for Water Supply, Alfred Deakin, had visited California in

1885 and seen the miracles wrought by two men, George and William Benjamin Chaffey. Deakin's visit took place against the background of a drought that had lain over northern Victoria since 1877, and he was sent to investigate irrigation in California. There the Chaffeys had developed a privately owned irrigation system which had brought into production previously barren land and so advanced the growth of California's fruit industry. Deakin was accused later of inviting the men to come to Victoria although there is doubt that he so did; but he did assure George Chaffey, who had arrived in Australia by this time, that the colonial government would make a land grant. Although the matter was by no means settled, William sold off the brothers' California interests and caught a ship to Victoria.

In 1888 they were allocated 250,000 acres on condition that they spent £300,000 over twenty years. The land concerned was the Mildura run, which was the largest squatting run in the region. Before the depredations of the rabbit, it had supported 80,000 sheep, but only twelve people. The decline caused by the rabbit had led the runholder to ruin, and the land had been seized by the bank. One day George Chaffey came to see the run, located 262km from the nearest railhead and typical Mallee country; he looked at the river banks and closely examined the flowers and shrubs which had been grown about the house where water had been available, and then decided this was the land he wanted. Deakin brought an enabling bill to the Legislative Assembly in Melbourne but the Chaffey critics were many, describing the Americans as 'cute Yankee land grabbers'. Before the Mildura issue was resolved, the South Australian government offered the Chaffeys an equivalent parcel of land in that colony, after which the brothers selected land on the Murray near Renmark. With both acquisitions, the two Americans now had 500,000 acres at their disposal.

The Mildura scheme required a huge pumping operation on the banks of the Murray, and 200 miles of channelling, much of it concreted. The land bloomed. A reporter for the Melbourne Leader travelled to the area in 1894 and reported that in the Mallee areas outside the scheme there was hardly a sign of life. The only break in the monotony of the Mallee was the occasional selector's mail box, an empty case nailed to a tree. By contrast, Renmark (which was the site of another Chaffey irrigation settlement) was noted for its good houses , its 'fruitful gardens of peach and olive, and the apricot and citrus fruits, as the lemon and orange are called'. The correspondent had visited Renmark eighteen months previously when it had looked like a railway construction town, but by this second visit the place looked as if it were there to stay. There he met George Chaffey, who showed him peaches grown from Californian seed and looked at the 'wonderful sight' of hundreds of fruit trees. Mildura by this time had a population of 3,500 (there were now 1,100 people living at Renmark) and, despite the economic depression which had affected all of Australia, was growing rapidly. The writer did find the long rows of peach and apricot trees monotonous and the wire rabbit-proof fences anything but picturesque, but this was more than compensated by the fact that in another year San Mateo was expected to have a first-class claret ready for the market.

It did not end well for the Chaffeys. They were hit like everyone else in Victoria by the collapse of the land boom in Melbourne. And there were plenty of settlers in their areas that wanted to see the back of the Chaffeys. By 1893 the government had set up the Mildura Irrigation Trust to take over the operation and a few months later Chaffey Brothers Limited went into liquidation. Of the land they had been granted, 438,000 acres was still unsold. George went back to America but William stayed on, stayed in the horticulture business and became the first Mayor of the new borough of Mildura.

But they left a legacy.

By 1920 land which had originally been offered at two and sixpence an acre was, even with a water rate of between forty-five shillings and £3, worth £80 an acre for vineyards in full bearing. Every settler had his racks and trays for drying raisins, sultanas and currants, and those who dried apricots, peaches, pears and prunes had their sulphur houses. The packing sheds with their whirr of machinery, along with the water-pumping stations, were the main features of the town. Irrigation schemes spread over the region and in 1921 it was reported that farms in the Murrumbidgee irrigation area were producing six or seven cuts each year' of lucerne.

Drought and depression

The irrigation areas solved the water problem locally, but for the rest of Australia drought has been a common and persistent nightmare. One meteorologist (J.C. Foley, Australian Bureau of Meteorology) who has made a study of Australian droughts compiled a thorough list. Governor Phillip recorded the drought which bedevilled the first two years of white settlement. Drought struck the infant New South Wales colony again in 1798, 1803, 1809, and then there was a severe one in the years 1813-15, when large numbers of stock died and wheat fetched £2 a bushel. Several dry patches followed over the next decade, and then there was another severe drought in 1827 when Lake George dried up. In 1829 the Darling River dried up. Another drought between 1837 and

1839 brought water shortages to Sydney and horse races were held on the dry bed of the Murrumbidgee River.

But worse was to come, and it was in the form of the great drought of 1895-1903. A highly detailed account was published in the *Agricultural Gazette of New South Wales*, when it gathered together the reports from inspectors of stock, inspectors of conditional purchases, district land surveyors, foresters and managers of department farms.

Mr D.A. Morgan , inspector of stock for the Wentworth District, wrote that he believed that the troubles had begun ten years before when eight inches of rain fell between 10 and 29 December 1894. He said that the rain had beaten down a lot of good grass, had silted up tanks and brought up a lot of useless weed. In his area, scrub-cutting to feed animals had been resorted to as early as June 1895, and settlers particularly missed the use of low scrub which had been eaten out by the rabbits. But the farmers cut whatever scrub they could find, and the sheep were prepared to eat most of it. By the end of 1897 the Wentworth district had lost 273,000 sheep from the 1894 population of 628,000. There was then some amelioration in the weather and stocks were partially rebuilt, and in 1900 particularly there was some useful rain. Then came disaster in 1902, when the drought worsened. That year the district's animal population fell by 515 horses, 333 cattle and 170,000 sheep. One run which formerly carried 70,000 sheep had only 5,000 left by 1902, while another stockholder had only 2,500 of his original 35,000 sheep.

Joseph Rochfort, inspector of stock at Jerilderie for twenty-seven years until his death in 1922, in 1902 still had stark memories of the 1876-7 drought, which had been assuaged by the fact that in 1875 the district had one of its best years ever and there was a residual supply of stock feed. No such luck this time. In the current drought, he wrote, scrub had kept much stock alive. Saltbush was a good source of feed for horses and cattle, but sheep killed it outright by eating all the leaves they could reach, making the plant top-heavy; then the brittle stem would break, and the sheep would finish off the leaves they could not previously reach. Mr W.H. Lee, surveyor at Wagga Wagga, wrote that handfeeding by purchased fodder had been economically ruinous to the farmers who had tried it, and that storage of fodder and hay during good seasons should be considered. He argued, too, that the then current practice of stripping the wheat and burning off the straw should be abandoned, as the straw would be a good stand-by in cases of drought.

Osborne Wilshire, district forester at Deniliquin, had formed the opinion that wide scale ringbarking and felling of timber in New South Wales had contributed to the decline in rainfall, and the practice of ringbarking trees right up to the watercourses meant that these streams and rivers did not hold water as long; any rain caught in the smaller creeks was subject to more rapid evaporation.

The Glen Innes and Tenterfield districts were not badly drought affected, but suffered nonetheless because they were overrun by starving stock from other areas.

In the Clarence River district where maize was the main crop, the hill crop failed by about 90 per cent. The best result for maize and other crops was obtained by ploughing deeply, harrowing to a fine tilth and keeping the cultivators going as frequently as possible, so preventing the formation of a hard surface, thus enabling the soil to retain what little moisture it was able to absorb. The manager of the Belindigarber experimental farm was another who stressed the need in future to store water and fodder, not to overstock, and that some trees on each property should be spared from ringbarking. The need for water conservation was also on the mind of the surveyor at Grafton, and he was concerned particularly with the necessity of fencing dams. There had been a number of cases of cattle being unable to extricate themselves when they were in a weakened condition and had become stuck in the boggy edges of dams where the water level had fallen.

Whatever the strictures of the experts, there seems little doubt that the drought of 1895-1903 was of such severity that the average farmer, preoccupied with day-to-day existence, could barely have been expected to make proper provision for its effects.

Its prolonged existence left the inland stock routes littered with dead cattle. Temperatures soared beyond the scale of thermometers. The Lachlan stopped flowing at Condobolin, and the Namoi at Gunnedah was a mere six inches deep. Few creeks on the south coast of New South Wales continued to run after mid-1897. It was a land of dying stock, dust and desperation. By mid-1898 water was being sent to Jerilderie for human consumption, let alone for stock.

By the middle of 1899 in central Queensland trains were running day and night, transferring nearly a million sheep from the great stations beyond Winton to the coast. As 1900 began, the pastoralists hoped that rain might relieve their situation, but January, then February and March, passed and the time for the wet season had gone with it. What stock remained was scattered along the isolated patches of feed. There were a few showers in July, and some runholders began railing stock back home, even though only three sheep had survived from each nine which had been railed away the previous year. Then 1901 passed with no further sign of substantial rain. Instead, dry, high winds swept over the country, with dust storms and whirlwinds in their wake. So the pastoralists had once again to rail stock back to the coast, but so weak were the animals now that fodder camps were organised along the tracks so that the stock could manage to reach the railway. And the relief country on the coast was itself beginning to dry up.

After the great drought of 1895-1903, Australian farming recovered but there was constant fear of another big dry. In 1907, at Goorimpa, in northwest New South Wales, teams work at excavating a new storage dam.

National Library of Australia

In inland areas, the winds dried up remaining waterholes and silted up tanks. Even the hardy ironbark trees began to die. Worse was to come. In 1902 many runholders and selectors could hold out no longer and walked off their land, even though banks avoided foreclosing wherever they could. In July there were more hot winds and bone dry weather; there was storms, but no rain. Afterwards the wind dropped, there was not a breath of air and all over the land hung a haze of heat. In 1903 again there was no wet season. There was a little rain in March but then hurricane gales destroyed the young grass shoots. By this stage, few women remained on the properties still occupied. They had escaped to the cities and towns to avoid final madness and despair. One woman recorded that she could no longer bear the sheep standing outside the house looking at her when there was no water left.

Things were just as bad in Victoria. In 1902 the wheat yield was 1.29 bushels an acre, the lowest it had ever been. The average annual harvest was sixteen million bushels; in 1902 it was 2.5 million. In 1895 there had been total crop failure in northern Victoria. In 1896 there were major stock losses around Bendigo and no water from the Murray was available for irrigation. In 1897 there was no grass left in the Wimmera, and emus and kangaroos were starving. In 1898 sheep were starving to death within twenty-five miles of Melbourne. In 1901 water was carried by train to the Mallee and some settlers had to go twelve miles to collect their water, and by the following year there was no drinking water at all for people in the Mallee.

Further droughts were to follow, and they strike there as fiercely today as they did in 1900. Between 1913 and 1915 eight million sheep died in the Riverina; in 1915 the Murray River was reduced to a depth of one foot at Echuca and was beginning to dry up at Swan Hill. When Queensland was hit by drought between 1925 and 1927 the Warrego River dried up at Charleville, and temperatures soared over 100 degrees Fahrenheit day and night for a week at a time. The butcher at Quilpie had to travel 250 miles to find cattle to kill. In April 1926 many dead horses lay in the fields around McKinlay and Kynuna, the cotton crop was devastated and the Flinders River was dry. Thirteen trains a day were needed to carry fodder from Rockhampton and Townsville to inland areas.

The next great drought was that which befell Australia between 1945 and 1947.

The Namoi River dried up at Gunnedah and in May 1945 the dairy factory at Gladstone closed because it had no water. By 1946 Rockhampton could not produce enough milk for local needs, Cunnamulla had its third poor lambing season in a row and Queensland Railways was carrying 400,000 gallons of water each week to the badly hit drought areas. Still the rains did not come, as sugar production slumped and cane growers dug their withered crops into the ground. The dry just went on and on, with endless reports of stock losses, bare pasture land, rivers drying up, hay sheds empty, and even scrub exhausted.

Drought, apart from its immediate catastrophes, had lasting effects on the economy. It also exacerbated the effects of fluctuations in the British and European economies.

And then there was depression.

By 1890, the gold boom had passed and refrigeration had not yet totally revolutionised the meat industry, although the first frozen meat shipment had sailed from Sydney in November 1879 in the *Strathleven*. Wool was still the country's premier export and there were 90 million sheep roaming the pasture lands of Australia by the last decade of the century. Much of the wealth went to the squatters — some became millionaires from the wool boom — and from their efforts arose the great pastoral companies such as Goldsborough-Mort. In parallel, grain exporting was growing apace and the gold boom had laid down a substratum of established wealth and capital, at least in western Victoria.

But when the depression of the 1890s hit, it was not the squatter nor the Melbourne financier who was economically paralysed. Rather it was the outback farmers who were up to their ears in debt, and already in peril from the combined ravages of rabbits, overstocking and drought. A writer in the *Banker's Magazine* in 1892 described the 320-acre-man as one who 'toiled and sweated himself into premature old age, clearing, burning, and fencing from day — dawn to sunset, and at the close of his toilsome, cheerless life, he often finds himself still at the plough'.

Putting everything on four feet had, by the time of the 1890s depression, led to a massive wool surplus. But it was not the first, nor was it to be the last, crisis in the primary sector. The great crisis of 1841-4, which had been produced by lavish spending and over-lending, was a precursor to the collapse of the 1890s. In 1842, New South Wales had to pass a new Bankruptcy Act which allowed debtors to retain their freedom provided they surrendered their estates to creditors. In 1843 the Bank of Port Phillip, the Bank of Sydney and the Bank of Australia all closed their doors. With the collapse of wool, the settlers in those days before refrigeration did not have the alternative of sending their stock to the abattoir. The markets in Sydney were firmly in the hands of the wholesale butchers who combined to depress prices even in the good times. The settler driving his sheep or cattle to market would be met within two days' ride of Sydney by one butcher who would offer him a low price, which would naturally be rejected. A few miles along the road, another would offer an even lower price, a third butcher one still lower. The farmer would frequently turn around and go back to accept the original offer, only to be told that the offer was no longer good. The man, by this time in a desperate mood, would be inclined to then accept any offer made. Needless to say, the three or more wholesale butchers were acting in concert in a well-practised scheme.

One saving innovation of the 1840s, which came in very handy in times of economic recession, was the development of large plants to boil down the carcasses of sheep and render them into tallow. The carcass would be cut up into large chunks, which were thrown into cast iron pans, boiled and the fat skimmed off. The meat was placed in presses and the last residue of tallow squeezed out, the residual meat then being sold for pig feed.

But while the settler of the 1840s could sit it out until times got better, eating mutton and damper and drinking pots of tea, the depression of the 1890s had a new element, because by this time a great deal more capital was required if you wanted to be, or continue to be, a grazier. Properties had to be fenced and land was transformed into freehold as the colonial governments increased the pressure for closer settlement. The squatter who could not adjust to the new times, or more importantly did not have the capital with which to adjust, was pushed off his land just like the small selector who had mismanaged his opportunity. Squatters and others who had paid too much for their land found that when wool dropped to eight and a half pence a pound there was no alternative but to quit. In South Australia alone during this period 30,000 square miles of land were abandoned.

Another factor which was now important was that most large properties were heavily dependent upon hired labour. The day of the cowed convict or ticket-of-leave man was gone. The shortage of labour in the rural sector during the gold rushes of Victoria and Queensland had meant that those who stayed behind had been able to parley for much higher wages, and these men established a much better standard for the hired farm-hand, although it was still a hard life for many. This, together with the drought conditions of part of the 1880s and the consequent shortage of money among many pastoralists, led inexorably to the shearers' strike of 1890.

One of the first great industrial disputes in Australia was the 1891 shearers' strike which broke out the Queensland town of Barcaldine after pastoralists sought to lower their wage costs by bringing in non-union labour, the Shearers' Union having been formed in Ballarat in 1886. The tools of the trade are amply illustrated in this undated photograph from New South Wales. National Library of Australia.

National Library of Australia

The shearers' strike

The shears had gone 'click' for 100 years, but it was not until 1889 that light, mechanised versions became available. Many shearers did not like the new equipment (just as their successors ninety years later in 1983 would come to oppose wide-comb shears), but that was not the real source of the problem. Before 1890, the general rate for shearing was seventeen shillings and sixpence per 100 sheep, although the employer could reduce that to fifteen shillings if he considered the work had not been done satisfactorily, a system which led to many, and bitter, disputes. There developed among the runholders a blacklist of men who resisted attempts to reduce payment, but the shearers got around this simply by changing their names.

The contract under which the shearers worked ensured that once they, or the shed-hands, were taken on, they were virtual prisoners until the job was finished. They could not leave midway through the job without incurring a heavy financial penalty, and what they earned was partly eaten up by the price of stores – rations had to be bought from the station store at whatever price the owner set. Accommodation was generally poor, consisting typically of slab huts with no windows and bare earth floor and with tiers of bunks on each wall. Sanitation was either nonexistent or extremely primitive.

The success with which the miners had organised into unions had not been lost on the shearers. The Shearers' Union had been formed at a meeting at Ballarat in 1886 and the squatters, who saw the new organisation as a direct challenge to their freedom, retaliated by setting up the Pastoralists' Union. It was when the pastoralists set out new levels of wages, all of them lower than the previous season of 1889, that the shearers decided to strike. Strike camps were set up throughout Queensland where the men banded together to hold out against the employers. A reporter from Melbourne's *The Age* reported that the camps were the closest thing to a home that many of these men had ever had, and 'in the little canvas tent or the gum bough shelter there is at least some kind of ownership and the owner is for that time his own master'. Life was primitive still, and some of the men broke the law by raiding Chinese market gardens for vegetables, but conditions were nowhere near as bad as they had been when working on stations like Kiacatoo. There, the *Queensland Observer* reported, the shearers had been expected to take their drinking water from a pool which was polluted by waste from the shearing shed and had been fouled by sheep and cattle. Many of the shearers suffered from persistent dysentery as a result.

The employers retaliated to the strike by offering the vacant positions to non-union men from Victoria (who were 'free labourers' or 'scabs', depending upon which side you were on), a move which led to a great deal of violence.

After a meeting of shearers at Barcaldine, 200 shearers rode to Clermont to intercept a trainload of non-union workers. While one party tried to uncouple the carriages on the train, another unsuccessfully tried to saw through the girders of a railway bridge. When the Queensland Government despatched troops to the troubled areas, the soldiers spent much of their time galloping off to false alarms. Some of the more violent strikers set fire to woolsheds and crops, and one of the leaders suggested they arm themselves with sharp shears mounted on poles.

By mid year the strike collapsed but, while the employers were able to dictate wages and conditions in the short term, the strike gave great impetus to the labour movement. At the next general election in Queensland fifteen Labor members were elected.

Farrer and his hybrids

Meanwhile, for the agriculturalist, things were beginning to improve. By the turn of the century wheat had become an important part of the Australian economy. The great drought apart, the land was being tilled, even in the pioneer fringe regions. The Mallee was a prime example. In 1879 a Royal Commission had described the country as 'sand, scrub and Mallee below, the scorching sun and bright blue sky above, and not a sound to break the solemn silence. In a journey of 100 miles from north to south not one solitary bird or living creature was to be seen ... All through this parched country there was no grass'. Thirty years later railways had opened up the no man's land, 6,000 people lived at Mildura, 550,000 acres were under crop and the strippers in 1912 took 5.7 million bushels of wheat.

In addition the agriculturalist was helped by improvement in wheat strains. William Farrer produced wheat varieties that allowed growers to escape the problem of rust. In 1889 the effects of rust attacks had been disastrous in the eastern states; in South Australia £1. 5 million worth of wheat had been lost through rust. Victorian flour millers had to import wheat that same year and the next year the colony's government convened the first of its conferences on the rust problem.

Farrer, who had lost heavily in mining ventures and then became a surveyor, had decided to attack the rust problem on his property near Queanbeyan in New South Wales. He determined to apply himself to developing new wheats that could complete their growing cycle without being attacked by the rust parasite. There had, in Australia, been no previous attempts to improve the quality of wheat, even though it had always been low in gluten content. Between the time of his resignation from the NSW Department of Lands in

1886 and his appointment in 1898 to that colony's Department of Agriculture as a wheat experimentalist, he derived no income other than that earned from scratching a living off the land.

Farrer spent years selecting the best strains from existing varieties, because he was concerned that they not be lost. He developed hundreds of new varieties, all tested and recorded. His life was one of long days under a blazing sun and sleepless nights pondering the problems. While he had to withstand his share of ridicule — he was called a crazy faddist — Farrer produced new varieties which were practically bunt-resistant. (As the *Australian Dictionary of Biography* points out, "Farrer was not so successful in producing rust-resistant varieties as popular legend credits him. Rather, his varieties were rust escaping due to their early maturity.")

Farrer argued that many areas of Australia were too dry for the bread wheats being attempted, and that the only way the farmers could turn a profit would be to adopt macaroni wheats. Gradually, from 1889, one hybrid after another was produced. One hurdle involved the flour millers: they were reluctant to abandon the wheat types with which they were familiar. Moreover, when crops of existing wheat strains were not affected by rust, they will still providing better yields than those devised by Farrer.

His most outstanding achievement was Federation wheat, which was evolved in 1901 to suit the Australian method of harvesting by stripper; it was a hybrid created by crossing a Fife-India wheat with 14A, a Purple Straw (the millers.' favourite). Federation was introduced in 1902 and accepted in leaps and bounds by farmers, producing uniformly good results in all parts of Australia. By 1909 (three years after Farrer's death) twenty bushels per acre in the Mallee were being recorded, thirty in the Wimmera — at least three or four bushels more than any other wheat, yielding an extra 1.5 million bushels more overall. In trials in South Australia Federation wheat proved the most productive in eight our of nine locations. Between 1910 and 1925 it was the variety most favoured by Australia's wheat growers. Eventually other strains replaced the ones he devised, but they all to some extent owe their existence to the man who began the revolution in breeding. It should be recorded, though, that Farrer's achievements were made possible by the faith held by Frederick Guthrie, the chemist with the New South Wales Department of Agriculture, who supported his efforts with encouragement and enthusiasm. In 1915 scientists in South Australia discovered that stinking smut could be controlled with copper carbonate.

The farmers were also helping themselves. Superphosphate was in common use by 1910. The farmer was becoming aware that the days of broadcast sowing were outmoded, and that the drill offered a much more efficient operation, reducing seed wastage and sowing the crop at a uniform depth in the soil. The drill meant that less seed was used because of reduced wastage. It also meant that a great deal of drudgery for both man and horse was eliminated, as it was no longer necessary to break up the soil to the extent required for broadcast sowing.

With the close of the nineteenth century the worst, for the moment, was over. Australian agriculture and pastoralism has been typified by optimism and bright hopes, if by nothing else. In 1909 — with memories of the great drought and the nightmare of the 1890s depression growing dimmer — Irish and Arnold, Crown Land specialists of Grafton, were promising potential settlers a rosy future in the Upper Clarence area. The pamphlet issued by the land agents gives a useful summary of the state of play in Australian agriculture at the time. For improved land in the Clarence River area, cane farms were worth between £30 and £35 an acre, mixed farms from £20 to £30, dairy farms £10 to' £15 and grasslands from £3 to £5 an acre. Unalienated Crown Land could be taken under conditional purchase for between ten shillings and a guinea an acre. For the settler a draught horse would cost £40, and his other costs would average:

Mares suitable for breeding	£35 to £40
Colts and fillies	£25 to £30
Springcart sorts	£15 to £25
Saddle sorts	£8 to £ 15
Ponies for sulkies or polo	£12 to 20
Dairy cows, young good sorts	£10 to 15
Steers, heifers (2 years old)	£2. 10 to £3. 10
Store bullocks	£5 to £6
Fat bullocks	£8 to 8. 10
Farm labourers	£1 a week and keep
Married couples	£78 to £104 a year
Boys for milking	7/to 15/a week

Freights to Sydney

Maize per bag	Ten pence
Potatoes per bag	Ten pence
Fowls per pair	Four pence
Pigs	1/to 4/
Eggs, per case	1/-
Butter/28 lb box	Sixpence

The early years of the century also saw a number of glowing pamphlets produced by the new Commonwealth Government, designed to attract migrants to Australia. While the examples were no doubt carefully chosen, they do leave us some idea of how farms of the day operated. One example was that of Mr Matthew Potter of Wagga Wagga, whose wheat production costs per acre were (in pounds, shillings and pence):

Ploughing	6s 0d
Cultivating	1s 9d
Harrowing (three times)	2s 3d
Seed	3s 9d
Manure	2s 6d
Drilling	1s 6d
Harvesting (one driver, one boy to sew bags, oil, five horses)	3s 9½d
Bags	3s 0d
Cartage to railway	0s 8d
Total	£1 5s 2½d
Returns:-	
26 bushels @ 3s 9d a bushel	£4 17s 6d
Net Profit:	£3 12s 3½d

Mr Norman Fry, of the Victoria district in Western Australia, supplied details of his 620 acres, of which wheat (the first crop) covered 200 acres. The land was ploughed four inches deep at a cost of eight shillings per acre with a three-furrow stump-jump plough. The land was neither harrowed nor rolled. The crop, which yielded twenty bushels an acre, gave him a profit of two guineas an acre. It was considered by the government agricultural experts that 200 acres of wheat was as much as a man could handle without outside help except at harvest time.

For the migrant who could not afford to buy his own land, there was the chance to farm on shares. The landlord provided cleared land, fenced and ready for the plough, and often helped the tenant to build a house. In turn, the tenant provided all the implements, horses and labour. The landlord would take half the harvest as rent, with each party providing their own bags for the harvested grain. The trend as the century moved into its second decade was toward diversification; no longer was it considered desirable to put everything on four feet.

Cotton farming had flourished in Queensland during the American Civil War, but once the United States returned to peace and full production the world price slumped again. By 1919 only 72 acres in Queensland were planted in cotton, but in 1902-21 world prices leapt and the acreage rose to 50,000. More than four times that area was planted in 1923-4. It was an industry particularly suited to a settler with a big family, the key to profitability being to eliminate labour costs at harvest time; returns were quick as the crop took only four and a half months to mature. Once the land was cleared most of the work could be done by the settler with the help of his children. One publication of the 1920s proudly shows a young girl who picked the impressive amount of 170 pounds of cotton in one day.

Harvesting hops in Tasmania. The island state was the principal producer of the crop. The first successful hop crops to be grown in Tasmania were planted by William Shoobridge in what is now North Hobart. In 1869, the Sydney Morning Herald reported that Shoobridge had 70 acres of hops under cultivation and that, in the surrounding area, his neighbours had planted a further 315 acres.

National Library of Australia

Hop growing was flourishing in Tasmania and Victoria, where there were rich loamy valleys sheltered from high winds. Of the two states, Tasmania was the principal producer of hops. In 1921 a planter could reap £6,000 from forty acres of hops. The only deterrent to the prospective hop grower was the high cost of starting up. The trellises required a great deal of expensive imported wire. It was customary to nip the vines in the first year so that there was no crop, early returns being obtained from planting potatoes, beans or tobacco between the rows.

Share cropping was an increasingly popular method by which people became established on to the land. John and Robert Boshier, who came from Wiltshire in 1910 as assisted immigrants, landed in Sydney with less than £10 between them. Their first move was to get a job on a farm at Inverell at £1 a week each and keep. They worked on wages for six months, and were then offered the cultivation of part of the farm on the half-share system outlined above. They did well, and in January 1913 rented a farm of 528 acres and ran it with a mixture of dairying, wheat and maize. It was a hard struggle but they persevered. In 1915 they gave up dairying and went in for a few sheep, and their position was gradually improving. After renting for six years they were in a position to buy the farm at Inverell on which they had originally been employed. By 1923, even after battling through a drought, the Boshiers could boast that their farm was one of the best in the Inverell district. They had both married Australian-born girls and between them had seven children.

The Australian dream of prosperity on the land was still live.

Chapter 5

Sugar and Blackbirding

Kanaka workers are allowed to pause for the camera in a typical Queensland sugarcane field.
John Oxley Library.

WHEN ANTHONY TROLLOPE journeyed around the country areas of Queensland in the 1870s he noted the considerable level of debt in which the squatters there had involved themselves. On some stations the interest on bank loans amounted to 20 per cent, enormous for those times. But what Trollope saw was a long way from Queensland's beginnings.

The penal colony established at Moreton Bay in 1824, and removed to the present site of Brisbane in 1825, was designed to restrain the worst recidivists from New South Wales. When these first whites arrived, Queensland had an Aboriginal population of probably about 100,000. Those of these original inhabitants living in the area of the penal settlement did not welcome the intrusion, and there were a great many clashes between the two races. During the life of the convict settlement anyone who had no connection with it was prohibited within a radius of fifty miles but, with the rundown of the prison in the late 1830s and the dwindling number of convicts, this isolation became very difficult to enforce.

The pressure from free settlers was inevitable once the explorer Allan Cunningham had set out overland from the Hunter River and discovered the highly fertile Darling Downs. He reported to Sydney that there existed lush grasslands and a good water supply and, by 1840, the first squatters had reached the area. The land rush dealt the final blow to the penal colony and it was closed in 1842. Queensland was for the independent farmer. The squatters of the Downs soon established a tight little community, which has survived to this day. Trollope's first impression of the Darling Downs was that the squatter hardly lived the life of the bushman. On some of the stations as many as 200,000 sheep were shorn, and the squatter had plenty of brandy and his wife many numbers of dresses purchased from the city stores.

In most cases despite the towering debt hovering over the landowner, Trollope could not imagine a happier life than that of the squatter:

> The sense of ownership and mastery, the conviction that he is the head and chief of what is going on around; the absence of any necessity of asking leave or of submitting to others these things in themselves add a great charm to life. The squatter owes obedience to none, and allegiance only to the merchant who asks no questions so long as the debt be reduced or not increased. He gets up when he pleases and goes to bed when he likes. Though he should not own an acre of land around him, he may do what he pleases with all he sees. He may put up fences and knock them down. He probably lives in the middle of a forest his life is always called life in the bush and he may cut down any tree that he fancies. He has always horses to ride, and a buggy to sit in, and birds to shoot at, and kangaroos to ride after. He goes where he likes and nobody questions him. There is probably no one so big as himself within twenty miles of him, and he is proud with the conviction that he knows how to wash sheep better than any squatter in the colony. But the joy that mostly endears his life to him is the joy that he need not dress for dinner.

Trollope noted that, when he visited Queensland, six of the seven ministers of the colony's government were squatters. The power of the squatter was such that, when the railway reached Dalby on the Darling Downs, the lines bypassed the township itself and instead terminated at the gates of the largest wool-producing property in the district.

Besides its substantial pastoral industry, Queensland quickly became known for its tropical and sub-tropical agriculture. Apart from the period of in indentured Pacific Islander labour (discussed below) Queensland's cotton and sugar cane areas were unique in that they were the only ones of any substance in the world worked by white labour.

If you look at the early history of cotton it is clear that a large labour-intensive sub-tropical crop was hard to farm economically. Cotton was first planted in Queensland in 1860, but it was not until the American Civil War created a worldwide shortage that Australian planters were able to make any headway; in 1870, they had 14,000 acres planted in cotton. But by 1887 there was no cotton being grown any longer, the Americans having resumed full production by then. The next fillip (for Queensland) came along in the form of the boil weevil which had ruined vast areas of cotton crops in the southern states of America. This pest had migrated from Mexico in 1892 and gradually spread across the cotton-growing areas of the United States in the following twenty years, reaching the zenith of its affect in the early 1920s. The Queensland state government, to help promote replanting in the light of this demand across the Pacific, gave a bonus of five and a half pence per pound of cotton delivered to the nearest railway station. In 1917, 133 acres of cotton were under cultivation, but by 1919 it was down to 73. Then came the spurt, with 1,967 acres in 1921 and 7,000 acres in 1922.

Sugar transformed the sub-tropical areas of eastern Australia, but other crops were important there, too. This 1912 photograph shows pineapples being harvested at Woombye, about 100km north of Brisbane.

John Oxley Library

As for sugar, it was sold at a minimum price in Australia which was maintained at a level to keep each part of the industry solvent. By 1928 sugar and other tropical crops were making a substantial contribution to the state's economy, being worth:

Sugar	£7,209,778
Bananas	£960,000
Maize	£802,349
Pineapples	£225,413
Cotton	£213,832

The crucial factor, though, about Queensland was that the various forms of agriculture and pastoral ism were complementary. In other words, they each used different areas and types of country that were particularly suited to them. For example, those areas planted in sugar, which were normally close to the coast, in the river valleys and on the slopes of smaller hills, might otherwise have remained unused, at least for several decades. Quite distinct areas with high crop specialisation distinguished Queensland's agriculture. For example, at Edgecumbe in 1928, 96 per cent of the land was planted in cane, with cotton accounting for 0.01 per cent and bananas for 0.25 per cent. At Port Curtis cotton covered 64 per cent of cropping land, with only nine per cent in sugar. Oddly enough, the farther north one went and the greater the specialisation, the lower the yield became. In the more temperate sugar cane areas across the border in New South Wales, the cane production for 1919-28 showed an average yield was, on average, a third higher per farm than in Queensland.

Bananas, too, proved a staple crop in Queensland, and here a load is leaving the farm in 1925.

John Oxley Library

But while sugar flourished because of its subsidies and protection, cotton never got the same hold because it could never compete with the farms of the U.S., Egypt and India. Both crops depended more upon politics than climate or soil.

The beginnings of the sugar industry

The first substantial attempt to cultivate sugar in Australia sugarcane had been brought on the First Fleet but attempts to grow some in Sydney were not successful was made in 1819 when a missionary, John Gyles, approached Governor Macquarie with the idea of investing in a plantation at Port Macquarie. Despite Gyles's prediction of an annual production of 500 tons of sugar and 32,000 gallons of rum, Macquarie had not the money to fund this vision.

The real founder of the sugar industry was probably Thomas Alison Scott, who had experience of cane growing in Antigua and Tahiti. He was placed on a government salary in 1823 to cultivate cane at Port Macquarie, where some had already been planted. By 1824 he was able to send the first samples of sugar to Sydney, and later that year a bottle of rum. However, the experiment was the victim of politics, and in 1828 Scott was dismissed by Governor Darling and the cane abandoned.

From 1861, the possibilities of tropical farming were opening up as white settlers moved into northern Queensland. The great breakthrough came with the experiment undertaken in 1862 by Captain Louis Hope and John Buhot on property at Ormiston, near Cleveland, when they were able to extract a ton of sugar from twenty tons of cane. Two years later Hope opened Australia's first commercial sugar mill; he also brought the first Pacific Islanders to Queensland to provide labour on his plantation. By 1879, just sixteen years later, sugar had spread along the coast of Queensland to Cairns, the main concentrations being around the towns of Bundaberg and Mackay, north of Bowen, and around Ingham, Innisfail and Cairns. The boom was nicely, if inadvertently, timed to coincide with a period of high world prices for sugar. The canegrowers soon learned that it was advisable from a soil management point of view to grow other crops between the rows of cane, so that supplementary production of carrots and other vegetables provided a useful additional income.

The first mills were primitive affairs, and often did not improve on Captain Hope's own backyard method of extraction, frequently using twenty tons of cane to extract just one ton of sugar. There was a great deal of waste. One of the

first mills consisted of rollers made of ironbark, eighteen inches in diameter, the
rollers being driven by a horse. The extracted juice was boiled in open pans and
set aside for about a week to granulate. Then the molasses was separated from
the sugar by putting the mixture in V-shaped boxes, perforated with very small
holes through which the molasses, over a period of a further ten days, slowly
drained. Even when some of the larger mills were built, horse rather than steam
power was the norm, with four horses walking a circular path to drive each set
of rollers. Many of the smaller mills, too, were but 'juice mills', and extracted
the liquid only. This was then sent to a larger mill for completion of the process.
The inefficiency of the early period is seen by comparison of production figures.
In 1886, 166 mills produced 59,000 tons of sugar, or an average of 350 tons
each. In 1901, with consolidations into a smaller number of mills and with
conversion to steam power, sixty mills accounted for 113,144 tons produced,
or an average of about 1,900 tons each. By 1920 mill production was up to
175,000 tons. The other factor which contributed to more efficient production
was the extensive network of tramway lines in the canefields. In 1956 there
were 2,000 miles of 24-inch track, and in years of good sugar production these
lines carried more freight than the whole of Victorian Railways.

The demand for cheap labour

One of the reasons for the absence of Aboriginal labour in the sugar and cotton
sectors was that, while they had proved quite adaptable to pastoral work, the
indigenous Australians had no history or experience of cultivating crops. On
the other hand, Melanesians always had vegetable and fruit gardens on their
islands.

Before the days of large mills, sugar tramways and government subsidies,
there was believed to be only one way to make the cane fields pay — and that
was with cheap black labour. Hence the introduction of the kanaka, the Pacific
Island worker so called from the Hawaiian word for man. While it remains
a grim episode in the history of a state which has not always been known
for its liberal view of life, two points need to be made. First, the Queensland
labour trade was neither the first nor the worst example of the exploitation of
Polynesian and Melanesian manpower. Secondly, the treatment of the kanakas
varied greatly on the Queensland canefields, and a number of accounts exist
which suggest that many were treated tolerably well, if not generously, by their
white employers. And, while the forced return of the kanakas to their islands
after federation was unprincipled and characterised by many islanders being
sent to places other than their original homes, the labour trade did not leave a

lasting nightmare of communal hatred and suspicion. This, by way of contrast, was to be the outcome of the altruistic intentions of the British bequeathed to Fiji, where the importation of Indian workers was intended to avoid the exploitation of Fijians on the sugar plantations. That it did, at the expense of making the Fijians a minority in their own land.

The ubiquitous Ben Boyd, squatter, financier, trader and shipowner, had brought the first recorded group of kanakas to Australia in 1847, when he recruited sixty-five men from the New Hebrides (now Vanuatu) to come and work on his runs at Maneroo and at Port Phillip Bay.

The shortage of labour in the Australian colonies after the abolition of transportation has been recorded in earlier chapters. It was particularly acute in Queensland, the youngest of the eastern Australian colonies, at a time when it was considered that white men were totally unsuited to manual work in the tropics, and sugar at that time required a great deal of manual labour. By the turn of the century gradual mechanisation of hoeing, transport and ploughing made it easier to contemplate the idea of white men working in the tropical heat, but in the 1860s the land clearing, cultivation, planting and cutting had to be done by hand.

The first consignment of kanakas to Queensland actually came to work the cotton crops of Captain Robert Towns at his plantation on the Logan River. The Governor, Sir George Bowen, advised London of the event, describing Towns as a 'highly respectable and influential merchant and shipowner of Sydney'. Towns had been given useful experience of the labour trade when he had been involved in recruiting men for collecting sandalwood before taking up his land in Queensland. The ships then began to arrive regularly: the initial shipment of sixty-seven men for Towns aboard the *Don Juan* was followed by fifty-four on the *Uncle Tom* in July 1864, and the same ship returned in November with eighty men. More and more ships entered the trade, and in August 1867 the *King Oscar* berthed with 225 kanakas crammed aboard.

Ben Boyd's men had rebelled when they saw what they had to do in Australia (and southern New South Wales was a much cooler climate, too), and few of the islanders who followed to Australia felt much happier. In the early 1860s several ships had been engaged in recruiting or kidnapping natives to work in the sugar and cotton plantations in Peru, and this was little more than a slave trade; few of these unfortunates ever saw their island homes again.

While Bowen continued to assure London that the islanders were being well treated in Queensland, there were others in both the Australian colonies and in the New Hebrides who were not so credulous. There were many in the cities who saw it as little more than a slave trade, and the missionaries in the New Hebrides argued that not only was the trade stripping the islands of their able-bodied men, but that their period in Queensland turned them into 'dangerous' characters when they came home. Accounts of the time often refer to the antics of the 'free' or 'walkabout' kanakas, as the time-expired men were called, and to their addiction to alcohol and opium which made them a menace to the community. There were also stories of fights between kanakas and Aborigines, often resulting in deaths. In Britain, too, there was growing unease at the stories that were reaching the authorities in London, and the assurances by recruiting agents and ships' captains that all signatures were obtained legally and from volunteers counted for little. The number of cases of ships being attacked when they called at the islands was clear evidence that something very grave was afoot. The issue gained further attention when in 1870 the labour traders, or blackbirders, in search of a new pool of men, began to work the Solomon Islands. Two years later the British Parliament enacted legislation to license all recruiting ships, and naval vessels were sent to enforce the laws.

By this time the Queensland Parliament had already felt constrained to act. In 1868 it passed the first of many pieces of legislation designed to remove the worst excesses from the labour trade. On Towns's property the kanakas were housed in a large building lined with bunks which had room for two men each; they worked from six until eight in the morning, then again from nine to noon, with an hour's break (two hours in summer) after which they worked until sunset. They were each given a pound and a half of food a day, usually beef and rice, water to drink and enough tobacco to allow them to smoke continuously all day. On other properties, though, they were forced to live in humpies, the tops of which were made with cane tops and leaves. The 1868 Act specified that each Pacific Island worker was to be paid £6 a year, and provisions were set out for food and clothing. Each man was to receive one pound of beef or mutton, one pound of bread, five ounces of sugar or molasses and two pounds of vegetables each day, with a weekly allocation of one and a half ounces of tobacco, two ounces of salt and four ounces of soap. Even so, they were still a lot cheaper than white workers.

Over the next decade the British tightened their control over the labour recruiters with laws which took on greater responsibility for the welfare of the island peoples. The Premier of Queensland, Samuel Griffith, had sought to meet the demands of the anti-kanaka lobby by passing legislation which provided that no more such workers would be allowed into the colony after 1890. Apart from the humanitarian aspects, Griffith and his followers felt that the easy supply of black labour made it possible for the large plantations to resist the cutting up of their land into smaller farms; nor did they want a growing population of blacks — this was the era of strident insistence on a 'white Australia'. The reformers had as their partners the labour movement, which wanted its members to have the pick of jobs, not to be undercut by black labour. In 1901, as the new federal government was moving to deport the kanakas, a *Worker* editorial alleged that the islanders were 'taking bread out of white men's mouths' and that they contaminated the white races, the latter assertion made in the face of almost non-existent miscegenation.

The growers, naturally, did not want their pool of cheap labour to disappear. In 1905, the year before the final deadline set down by the federal government (still in Melbourne) for the deportation of all kanakas, the Rockhampton *Daily Record* staged a last-ditch stand. It argued that the only export crop Queensland had was sugar, that in 1903 export trade was worth £1.6 million and that the deportation of the kanaka would be the ruination of the industry. By all means, the paper argued, keep out the Chinese, Japanese and other coloured races, but allow the kanakas to stay. It urged several precautions, including restrictions on where they could work, a ban on intermarriage and a refusal to give them any 'Australian status'. After all, the farmer would not find any more attractive labour prospect, even though various laws had increased the islanders' wages. 'They are the most tractable, the easiest managed, and give the best results,' the writer noted, which was a good deal more than could be said for the white worker. It reported on the situation at Mossman Mill where in a year 400 men had to be employed to maintain a basic workforce of 150, because after pay-day 20 per cent of the whites would disappear, and those that stayed would not work in the fields.

Other accounts attest to the diligence of the islanders. They gave the impression of preferring to work in gangs and were 'docile' under discipline. One farmer, Charles Eden, recorded that he employed twenty 'boys' whom he found trustworthy and reliable, also adding that they were docile (again), laborious and light-hearted. Most of their work was concerned with trashing (stripping the cane of unwanted leaves and keeping down the weeds) and in their spare time they grew taro and hunted emus and other native fauna. Eden and others apparently trusted them with hand weapons. Another account recorded the case of a planter who learned the language of his workers, and rather than put them on rations allowed them a reasonable supply of beef, sweet potatoes, yams, corn meal, green corn, arrowroot, sugar, molasses, milk and tobacco. The settlers in central Queensland found that all these crops grew easily, as did many English vegetables such as spinach, cabbage and carrots.

Anthony Trollope saw nothing wrong with the system. He wrote:

> They are always clean, and bright, and pleasant to be seen. They work well, but they know their own position and importance. I never saw one ill-used. I never heard of any such ill-usage. The question to my mind is whether they are not fostered too closely wrapped up too warmly in the lambswool of Government protection. Their dietary is one which an English rural labourer might envy.

Unfortunately, the kanakas had little opportunity to publish their views of the experience, nor were the less enlightened employers inclined to set down their practices for posterity. What one can say is that while the method of recruitment and the concept itself, too, were totally reprehensible even by the standards of late Victorian Britain and Australia, the picture is not one of unrelieved misery.

What is certain is that the sugar industry would never have made the progress it did without the cheap labour provided by the Pacific islanders and other 'coloured' workers. In 1884, as one example, the Pyramid Mill at Mulgrave employed 35 Europeans, 100 Chinese and 87 kanakas. If it had had to employ 222 whites, it would probably have been put out of business very smartly — if not by the cost of white wages, then by the patent unreliability and slothfulness of many of the European workers.

The Queensland sugar industry survived the end of kanaka labour owing mainly to bounties and monopolies, and to heavy tariffs on imported sugar, especially that produced cheaply in Java by the native people there, and in Fiji by indentured Indian labour.

The last canecutter

The increasing mechanisation of both field work and the mills was making the imported labour gradually redundant. Federation forced other changes. On the plus side, it did away with internal restraints on sugar sales. The Victorian Government had levied a £5 per ton tariff on the sugar, and reformers of the labour trade argued that if that import duty were abolished then the kanaka labour force could be dispensed with and the cane-growers could afford European workers. The sugar producers had already been exploited by the Victorians before the tariff was introduced. Not only were there sugar rings working in Melbourne conniving to keep the prices down (and which were happy to buy Fijian or Java sugar if it were cheaper) but the string of brokers, shippers and bankers all took a substantial slice of the price of sugar moving southwards from Queensland. Federation also meant, as mentioned earlier, that the liberal conscience had a conduit at last. One of the first acts of the new national parliament was to legislate to end kanaka labour by 1906. Only those kanakas who were old, married, owned freehold land, or would be imperilled by a return home would be allowed to stay.

Even with the plight of the unwilling workers brought from the South Pacific, there were still plenty of those who opted for the work, as with this group of Italian cane-cutters in an undated photo. The woman would probably have cooked for the team.

John Oxley Library

Anyway, there was no real fear that the sugar industry would collapse. A number of parliamentary acts, including the Sugar Works Guarantee Act 1893 and the Customs Tariff Act, had seen to that. The former ushered in the system of central mills, where larger factories provided economies of scale, while the break-up of the old plantations led to many smaller units (by 1956 the average cane plantation was fifty acres). Each of the new mills drew on about 800 planters, so there was a good spread of supply. In fact it was the system of central mills which most facilitated the transfer of sugar production from black plantation labour to the white farmer system. From 1901 until 1913 the system was helped along by a bounty paid on sugar produced by white labour, which was actually just a refund of the excise tax on all cane plantations. By 1913 the kanakas had all left (except for the exempted categories) and the Chinese been effectively forced out of the business by having no bounty paid to them. So there was no need for the bounty any longer. A further measure in the form of a £6 per ton tariff on imported sugar helped a lot, too. The industry flourished: Queensland produced 152,259 tons of sugar in 1905-6, 184,305 tons in 1906-7, 188,352 tons in 1907-8.

By the time the federal government's Royal Commission on the Sugar Industry reported in 1912, only six per cent of the nation's sugar production was produced by coloured labour, comprising some Chinese and the remaining kanaka labour.

The commission was, however, more concerned with the organisation of the milling and refining of the sugar. The milling was carried out by what was still known as the central mills, whose ownership rested with the growers. These mills were intended as co-operatives, but what had happened was that shares were concentrated in the hands of a minority of cane suppliers. The mills then supplied the raw sugar to the refining companies, of which there were only two: the huge Colonial Sugar Refining Company, and the much smaller Millaquin refinery (where a refinery had existed since 1882; it became part of Bundaberg Sugar in 1975). In effect, there was no competition, the Millaquin company falling into line with C.S.R. as the least troublesome way of doing business. The millers had no option but to supply the refiners — they could not export raw sugar in competition with the much cheaper Java product, and anyway C.S.R. was a large purchaser of raw sugar from both Java and Fiji. The Royal Commission concluded that C.S.R. 'must in the end get its way'.

That way was, not unexpectedly, to fix prices to its own advantage. The price was fixed so that it was neither so high that it encouraged Australian consumers to use imported sugar, nor so low that it would force the growers off their land. The screw was kept tightened, but with moderation.

Just as the millers had no one to sell to other than C.S.R. and Millaquin, the growers in each area had no choice of mill. The millers in their turn, the commission found, exploited the non-shareholder grower. Many of the mills paid the non-shareholder grower lower prices than they paid the shareholders, and the latter had the additional benefit of the annual dividend, a large part of which consisted of the profit made from the cheap cane bought from the non-shareholders. George Johnson of Mackay summed it up when he gave evidence that for him it was a question of take the price offered for his cane by the Double Peak Sugar Company or starve. The commission concluded that these growers were being paid a subsistence price, just enough to keep them in business until the next season.

C.S.R., which not only refined sugar but had other products including manure, acids and a distillery, succeeded in obtaining a High Court injunction to prevent the royal commission from examining its accounts. The commission's report commented on the veil of secrecy which clouded C.S.R.'s financial activities, and the company's methods of bookkeeping which made it impossible to disentangle the various sources of its profit.

If the growers did not receive a fair share, the worker in the Colonial Sugar mills was little better off. The report commented unfavourably upon the wages and conditions imposed: for example, in the washhouse the men working on the cane had to endure a humid atmosphere, wearing only loin cloths. The commissioners considered the conditions 'very trying', and the daily wage of seven shillings and five pence scant reward for hard and unpleasant work.

Prospective migrants in Britain were being sold a different story. *Empire Magazine* was telling of vast areas of virgin land in Queensland which were just awaiting the British plough, after which not only sugar would flourish, but also rubber, vanilla and tea. Maize, potatoes, root crops and fruit could all be raised to complement the main crop, and the example of one Ingham farmer who harvested eighty-five bushels of maize to the acre was quoted. A book offering guidance to migrants to Australia maintained that a good cutter could earn up to fifteen shillings a day. The way to make a future in Queensland, it advised, was for several men to form a gang and elect a leader who would then negotiate cutting contracts. Each man would earn £100 on average in the harvesting season, of which a third would go on keep. As it needed anywhere between £200 and £500 to get established on a small plantation, it would probably take up to six years before a cutter could save enough. But it was essential, too, that he spend that time working in the industry simply to learn enough to be able to run his own plantation. The new worker on the sugar fields would need, the book stated, a good pair of boots, puttees, warm flannel shirts, woollen singlets and a sun hat.

But, after the departure of the Pacific Island labour and the forcing out of the Chinese by means of the bounty on white-grown cane, the growers were largely dependent on a nomadic group of cutters which each year would gather from all parts of Australia, and even from New Zealand. They would sign on at the mills or the canegrowers' halls, and were housed in galvanised-iron barracks. The first week was the worst as even the most experienced cutters began with soft hands and flabby muscles. Apart from the cutting, the men had to carry the harvest to the nearest railway wagon. Most of the fields were served by portable branch lines laid off the main track of the tramways, so that the cutters also had to carry and lay the portable track to where they were working.

Up until 1939 the cane was largely green when cut, but the shortage of labour during World War II saw most of the crop being burned before harvest, to make it easier to cut. In 1957 bulk handling became uniform, which put the baggers out of a job.

In 1971 the universal acceptance of mechanical harvesting put the last canecutter out of work, too.

Chapter 6

The Drover's Dream

The horses rest and the drover's dog gets to slake its thirst with water poured into the man's hat. This photo was taken in 1915 at Adavale (west of Charleville) in Queensland.

John Oxley Library

EARLY IN 1985 a newspaper account appeared reporting what was headlined as 'the last great cattle drive'. The story marked, and celebrated, what it called 'the old national' spirit which had been typified by the stock routes which had criss-crossed the interior of the continent since white people began occupying the land. The drover in the article, Viv Walsh, had decided that the trip with 850 head of cattle from Queensland to the Hunter Valley was perhaps going to be his last and that, with his retirement, no longer would Australians see vast mobs strung out along the roads, walking to new pasture or the market. Like their predecessors, the cattle make their way slowly, averaging about six miles a day, the drovers careful not to have their charges lose too much condition. The only difference between the overlanding of today and that of a century ago is that the traditional stock routes have disappeared and now the mobs walk the edges of macadamised road, and that the drovers have trucks to carry their supplies rather than pack-horses. Those stock routes which have survived, like the Birdsville track, are now used not by the drovers but by heavy trucks carrying cattle to the railhead.

The first stock routes were determined by the availability of water and feed as the pioneers moved inland with their sheep in search of land. As soon as areas became settled, the stock routes changed from a flow of stock inland to populate the new farms to a coast-bound one of sheep on foot headed for sale, or more usually the wool clip going out by dray and bullock team. In October 1836 John Hepburn and others set out from a station on the Murrumbidgee to take stock to Port Phillip Bay, and Hepburn found that both sides of the river were lined with squatters. It took them three days to get from Gundagai to the Murray River, and they swam the stock across, and then took the track made by the Surveyor-General, Thomas Mitchell, to Port Phillip Bay. Two years later Hepburn took 1,650 sheep, with ten convicts to help, from southern New South Wales to Melbourne. At the Murray he overtook another overlander, who had taken eight days to get his sheep across the river. The early drovers found autumn the best time of the year to move, and the Riverina became a popular holding place for cattle and sheep from further inland. The mobs would be moved in autumn, then held and fed in the lush Riverina pastures and sold over the whole year to provide a steady supply. The Birdsville track became a popular overlanding route in the 1880s when the railway being built to Oodnadatta reached Hergott Springs (or Marree, as it is now known). In fact, in 1980 when the old narrow gauge Central Australian Railway from Marree to Alice Springs was closed, the line to Marree from Port Augusta was retained for a while partly because of the cattle traffic still coming down the Birdsville by lorry (although it has now long since closed completely).

Overlanding has always been hard work, constant vigilance being essential to prevent stampedes when the cattle become unruly from a combination of heat, dust and flies. The earliest drives were often through virgin or barely explored territory. The first droving northward from Sydney took place in 1840 when sheep were overlanded to the Darling Downs in Queensland. In 1842 Joliffe and Hunter took 20,000 sheep to Wide Bay through unexplored country. Then, in the 1860s, Frank and Alexander Jardine took a mob to Cape York, at times passing through almost impenetrable forest, at one stage making five miles in four days, and being under daily attack from natives. In 1879 Nat Buchan delivered cattle to Glencoe and Wave Hill in the Northern Territory and the Ord River in Western Australia after overlanding from Queensland. In

1881 Warby and Smith drove 6,000 cattle over 3,000 miles from Queensland to the Northern Territory; it took eighteen months and in the Gulf country the stock was attacked by crocodiles. It did not get easier with time: in 1911 one mob of 5,000 sheep was being moved from Lucknow in Queensland to Avon Downs in the Northern Territory. At one point before they reached the Diamantina River the drovers had to negotiate thirty-five miles of waterless country. On the fourth day of this stage a small clump of trees came into view. The sheep bolted for the shade. As they piled on one another and the pressure of weight increased the sheep underneath suffocated. Of the entire mob, only 200 survived.

Drovers were not usually the kind of people to keep a record of their lives or feats, but one who did was Alexander Buchanan. With seven others, he set out from Sydney to take sheep overland to South Australia as a speculation. Buchanan kept a detailed diary of the trip, and it provides a wonderful record of early overlanding. They set out from Sydney on 11 July 1839. After five days, one of the drovers (an ex-convict) had run away and a man had to be on guard all night to watch for bushrangers. The country was well populated by mounted police, mainly to hunt down those bushrangers. Six miles from Goulburn they passed a chain gang of 200 men making a new road. After riding through Yass they had to make their way along an unformed track, the road going no farther. Each day began early as the horses had to be rounded up; they were hobbled each night to prevent their taking long steps, but even so they could stray for two miles in search of feed. On 26 July the men were up at daybreak but it took until nine o'clock for them to find all the saddle horses. The drays set out an hour earlier. After Yass the journey became even slower as the cart-horses had to be let out to feed in the middle of the day, the stop being made wherever there was grazing, there being no longer any commercial stables to provide feed. At Howe's property on the Murrumbidgee (the same property from which John Hepburn had set out for Port Phillip Bay three years earlier) the young entrepreneurs collected their 4,023 sheep for the journey to South Australia.

Eventually, with other sheep they had contracted to drive for another owner, the party had 13,000 animals on the trail. There was no time to stop and look after new-born lambs; on 21 September Buchanan recorded that he still had about 600 ewes ready to lamb, and that the lambs were killed as soon as they dropped.

As they passed beyond the last white-inhabited station, life became hard. The men were growing weaker from all their exertions, and the ground was bad — there were many large holes and a horse's legs could go down to its knees in them.

Drover W Golding's Camp

The day is over for the cattle as they settle to rest an overnight camp in Queensland. The photo is undated, but by the mid-1880s drovers were undertaking epic overland cattle droving trips covering vast areas of Queensland and Western Australia.

John Oxley Library

By the middle of October the party had reached the banks of the Lachlan River. They saw blacks every day at a distance, and within a few days the natives were coming up to the camps at night asking for food and axes. Meanwhile the men were growing impatient with the progress. On 24 October Buchanan recorded: 'One of the men gave me notice tonight that he could stand it no longer. I told him that if he did not work he could not expect to eat.' A few days later a group of blacks attacked the sheep with boomerangs and had to be driven off with musket fire. Then some of the men were attacked as the mob was being taken across the Darling River. In the fight guns proved more lethal than spears, and five or six of the Aborigines were killed before the attack was driven off. From then on there were frequent clashes with the blacks, and several were killed by gunfire. While in the settled areas the native men would normally take unattended stock, or attack a sole shepherd; in the unsettled regions the drover could generally expect more fierce and pressed assaults.

In 1870 Arthur Ashwin set out from South Australia to take 7,000 sheep and 300 horses to Port Darwin at the northern tip of the continent. In the party, there were nine white men, three blacks, twenty-five dogs and a year's provisions. Early on, kerosene was spilled and soaked a bag of sago; they decided to keep the sago just in case, which was as well, because before the journey was finished they ate it. By the time they reached the Finke River the sheep had travelled eighty miles without water, and had survived only because recent thunderstorms had produced some green feed. When the party reached the river it was dry apart from a salt waterhole, but that night there was rain and by morning there was more than six feet of water in the river.

Because there was no hope of crossing the Finke for probably a month, Ashwin and another man, one of the blacks, tracked back whence they had come looking for a mare which had been lost. It rained again and they found themselves separated from the rest of the men by a suddenly torrential creek which had been dry the day before. They swam across and made their way back to the Finke because it would have been impossible to travel further south with all the watercourses suddenly full of water.

A fortnight later Ashwin tried again and found the mare. After camping for five weeks, they decided to cross the Finke , by now a quarter of a mile wide and with water up to the men's armpits. The sheep had to swim, but once they had got the mob across the men found that the land was so swampy they had to camp for another six weeks. Life was made more trying by the presence of thousands of rats which each night attacked the food supplies.

Travelling north of Alice Springs they followed for a while the track made by the men building the overland telegraph, but soon they were on their own again. Then they encountered a group of blacks. When Ashwin was out with John Milner, the brother of the stockowner, one native ran up and smashed the young man's head with a club. The blow smashed the skull from the ear to the eye, and both eyes were out on John Milner's cheeks; he died soon afterwards. It was the first of several attacks, and the party was glad of the weapons it had brought.

Even as late as 1885-6, when Patrick Durack was part of a droving team taking 2,000 cattle from central Queensland to the Ord River in Western Australia, the Aborigines were considered a constant threat, and the drovers armed themselves well. But this particular epic journey suffered more from the normal depredations of the long duration of the trip and hostile country than from its native inhabitants. When they were approaching the Limmen Bight River, which debouches into the Gulf of Carpentaria, the thirsty cattle rushed the water. But the river was busy with alligators, and several of the drinking cattle were gripped by their noses and pulled under the water.

When eighteen-year-old William Bates was hired to help an overland trip between Port Phillip Bay and the then unsettled Mount Gambier in 1845, his task was to work the dogs so he had to walk all the way.

Oscar de Satge, who started overlanding in Queensland in the 1850s, beginning with taking cattle to the tallow works in Ipswich, found that a drover very quickly got to know the stock. He soon knew the 'rogue' or 'rowdy' of the mob who would, at a bend in the road, veer off toward a creek or other stock encountered on the journey.

At the end of the day's ride the routine would be to hobble the horses while one of the men — quite often blacks were hired to carry out these menial tasks — would light the fire and boil the billy for tea. Normal tucker was cold boiled salt beef and damper; when the beef ran out they would resort to damper alone.

One man would always ride ahead to give stations along the track notice that a mob was approaching. if it was a particularly large number of stock, they would be divided into two or more mobs, each with its cook and supply wagon and the two groups might not see each other until the end of the journey. The supply cart would go ahead of the shepherds and stop at a place fixed for the next night's camp. The cart driver would erect the tents and get everything ready for the men who would normally appear by midday, the sheep having been taken the set six or seven miles for that day. In the afternoon the drovers would make sure that the sheep were feeding. At night it was usual for two men to be on watch at anyone time, with fires being lit around the mob to keep the native dogs away, and the men would have to keep up a supply of fuel to the fires. On ope overland drive on which de Satge was employed, one small mob was abandoned by its drover. That night, while they were unattended, almost 1,000 were killed by dingoes.

If the sheep were well fed, most of them would lie down for the night, but if the camp area had not been well grassed then the mob would give trouble all night. They would in any case be uneasy as day broke, so that the men had to be up before it was light. First up was the cook, who would start frying mutton chops for breakfast.

Patrick Durack remembered the cattle camps of his overland journey with nostalgia. The camp at night had a glamour of its own, he wrote some years later. But if the beasts were uneasy, then it was an anxious night for the one who was on watch. There would always be some of the mob on their feet at night, and a few would move off to graze, and if the drover was not careful this would lead others to follow. What the drovers feared greatly was the sudden rush of cattle which precipitated a stampede. Usually it was never known what set off these stampedes, but some camps were disliked by the cattle and they did not settle all night. When the stampede started, the men would rush for their horses, and the night would be filled with the thunder of hooves, shouting and yelling in the dark, and the crack of stockwhips. The most dangerous part was for the man who rode to head off the leaders of the stampede, but for any of the drovers, a wild ride in the pitch black through tree-covered country with a mob in stampede was a perilous business. Most stampedes were stopped within a mile or so, but the worst part was that the cattle would lose their horns when they struck trunks or branches of trees, or their shoulders or legs would be broken.

Kidman was different

Most of the men who worked on the stock routes died or retired with little more than they began with, but one who broke out of the mould was Sidney Kidman, who became the leading outback figure of his day. By the time he died it was said that a mob of cattle could cross from north to south across Australia and never leave Kidman's land. It was a great exaggeration, but he did own 100,000 square miles of land when his empire was at its zenith, and he was the biggest horse-breeder and cattle-owner in the country.

Kidman was born in South Australia on 9 May 1857, and by the age of thirteen was employed as a cattle drover at ten shillings a week. He saved his money, bought a bullock team and set up as a carrier, carting supplies in the far west of New South Wales to and from Bourke, Tibooburra, Cobar and Wilcannia. Then he ran a butcher's shop in Cobar, attracted by the sudden growth of the town upon the discovery of copper. A legacy of £400 from his grandfather allowed Kidman to expand his trading activities, setting up a coaching operation and more buying and selling of stock.

During the drought of 1880 he rounded up abandoned stock, and then spent the £1,500 he made buying 3,000 horses and 500 cattle. He made sure he knew the land and was travelling constantly, looking at property and stock, buying and selling. His first station, Owen Springs southwest of Alice Springs, was bought in 1886. Gradually he bought a chain of stations toward both Broken Hill and the South Australia border, and then through the Flinders Ranges. By 1914 his land holdings were equivalent in land area to an area greater than Tasmania — hence the perception that traversing Australia would involved merely stepping from one Kidman property to another.

He also turned to good account the disastrous drought at the turn of the century. In 1903 Kidman rounded up straying mobs throughout northern and central Australia and made a profit of £40,000 from their sale. The money was poured back into acquisitions of both land and animals. When the 1914 drought struck Kidman lost 100,000 cattle and 50,000 sheep, but he had saved enough money to survive. By owning a string of properties, he always had some usable pasturage. At Guthrie he made a typically shrewd deal: he bought 10,000 sheep at seven shillings each, then wired to Adelaide asking £1 a head delivered there, which he got. On that occasion he made £6,500 profit. These deals enabled him to restock his properties quickly once the drought had broken.

Money helped in other ways. At the Monkira station in Queensland he bought out the ruined owner cheaply, drilled and found water and made this latest acquisition drought-proof. Another station which had been brutally hit by the drought was Carrandotta. Once it had held 100,000 sheep, 26,000 cattle and 2,000 horses, but after the drought of 1895-1903 the stock numbers were down to 18,000 sheep, 5,000 cattle and 800 horses. He restocked as soon as the rains came, and between 1903 and 1914 the property sent off 130,000 sheep and 30,000 cattle to the markets, plus a huge annual wool clip. In 1914 Kidman sold the property for a substantial profit. Another of his bargains was Coongry in South Australia; he acquired its 1,600 square miles for £2,990.

The Tinnenburra station in southern Queensland was begun as a cattle rearing operation but the high wool prices of the 1890s convinced the owner, James Tyson, to switch to sheep. So vast was the property that in 1895 Tyson had built at the then enormous cost of £7,000 this shearing shed, the largest in Australia. It had more than 100 stands — that is, positions for shearers.

A. Barton-Burke

The lure of northern development

Kidman understood that a combination of vast areas, cheap labour and easily managed stock was the way to make money out of the north. Plenty of people never learned that lesson, or, if they did, it was usually learned at great expense. It was long one of the persistent fables of modern Australia that the north of the continent provides a new destiny for the nation if only we could find some way to develop it (apart from mining, which does not usually bring development in depth in terms of associated industries and a whole societal infrastructure). As this new edition is being prepared, there is again talk along these lines. Perhaps this time it will succeed; after all, the perceptions regarding the Ord River scheme have mellowed over time.

Generations of dreamers have gazed at the vast expanse of territory across the northern third of Australia and expounded schemes to turn it into a highly productive region. If we don't use it, someone else will take it, has often been the claim, meaning that hordes of "Asiatics" (as they were called by the whites more than a century ago) will descend on our northern shores and immediately transform the region into a sea of rippling paddy fields or verdant grasslands. While it could certainly be said that cheap Asian labour would offer some financial inducement to attempt other than low-animal density pastoral enterprises, the fact is that when Asian labour has been introduced into the Northern Territory it has been a failure.

As we have seen, when the Chinese did try and produce sugar cane in Queensland (although they were possibly the one group of growers who might have been able to produce sugar at prices competitive with other countries and so avoid the need for tariff protection) they were squeezed out by the bounty given to white growers.

In the 1980s the Northern Territory government became involved in pilot and experimental schemes to widen the basis of agriculture. Its great success was to lobby for the completion of the long-promised (the Commonwealth made the pledge in 1911) railway link from Alice Springs to Darwin. Back in the 1980s, the politicians in Darwin argued that the railway would make pastoral production more economic since the stock could be moved more quickly. It seems, however, that it has been the miners rather than the pastoralists who will benefit most from the new steel road.

Various early attempts at settlement were made along the northern coast of Australia, but it was the men of money and influence in Adelaide who provided the first substantial impetus for northern development. They wanted South Australia to be the premier colony in Australasia and, with the close settlement of the southern portion almost completed, they began to look toward the Top End. The primary manifestation of this ambition was the building of the railway north from Port Augusta to Oodnadatta (it was to reach Alice Springs nearly thirty years after federation) and another line south from Darwin which eventually reached Birdum — the middle of nowhere — before coming to a halt.

In 1902 the South Australian Government published a report on the proposal for a landgrant railway to bridge the 1,063 mile gap between

Oodnadatta and Pine Creek (at which points the two railheads were in that year). It was a land of 'boundless resources', the government argued, and the railway would open up 334 million unalienated acres. It was proposed in a South Australian parliamentary act that the railway be offered to private enterprise and that, in return for constructing it, the successful applicant would be granted 75,000 acres of land for each mile of railway completed. It looked set to go ahead, and the act specified details of the railway, including the fact that the motive power was to be steam, perhaps because a contractor in Western Australia had opened a railway using horse-drawn wagons to save money. The company, having completed the Oodnadatta-Pine Creek section, would have been entitled to 79,725,000 acres of land, but the negotiations which led to the Territory being taken over by the federal government in 1911 ensured that the private-owned scheme did not get under way.

Nevertheless, the 1902 report is interesting because of the way it reflects the perceptions of the Northern Territory at that time. Where water-supply could be controlled — whether by dam, tank, well or artesian bore — failure was the exception for those who set themselves up in the Territory, it said. Cattle, sheep and vegetables would all thrive if water was available. The report was quite definite about the possibilities: north of Barrow Creek the Territory could sustain two million horned cattle. By way of proving the point, the report adduced the fact that Sidney Kidman, even in the worst days of the then current drought, had been able to despatch cattle each week from the Territory for the markets of the south. In another dazzling piece of prefiguration, the writers said that the southern half of the Territory would be highly suitable for sheep, once the railway came. It was too expensive to transport wire and fencing posts by camel, but trains could not only bring in fencing materials cheaply but take the fattened sheep and the wool on their return journeys. Then there could be ostrich farming, and 54 million acres of agricultural land, including substantial production of cotton. If the Commonwealth government in Melbourne would allow cheap Asian labour to enter the Territory, then rice would be viable, along with sugar, coffee, tobacco, rubber, jute and other crops.

Now, these beguiling ambitions are not repeated here just for the sake of a wry chuckle from the advantage of hindsight, but rather to illustrate the degree of hope and ambition which surrounded the question of northern development. The report was produced under the name of Simpson Newland, a former treasurer of South Australia and contained a great deal of material which showed that the notion of a well-watered, prosperous north was a commonly held one. For example, among the supporting documentation was a report reprinted from the *Allahabad Pioneer* — then one of the most influential English language newspapers of British India — of 27 November 1902 in which a Captain W. R. Creswell reported that his visit to the north of Australia showed that it was good territory in which to breed and train horses for the Indian Army. If a remount depot were established, he argued, it could manage to maintain a pool of 12,000 horses in northern Australia.

There were others who saw the same alluring prospects. In 1874 a German botanist, Dr M.G. Holtze, established the Botanical Gardens at Darwin, and demonstrated that sugar, bananas, pineapples, rice, coffee, cocoa, tea, pepper and cloves could all be successfully cultivated, at least in strictly controlled conditions. In 1891 the Governor of South Australia, the Earl of Kintore, visited Darwin, by which time Holtze's son was curator of the Botanical Gardens. Young Holtze argued to the governor that all that was needed was cheap labour, and that rice, tobacco, sugar and coffee would flourish. With coolie labour (it was proposed to bring Indians to Darwin) it was suggested that a ten acre plot of tobacco would net a £400 profit. In 1896 another government report urged the establishment of rice plantations on the South Alligator River, and sugar cane and other tropical agriculture along the Daly River.

When the Federal government assumed responsibility for the Territory in 1911 it pressed the leading authority on Australian farming of the day, Walter Campbell, the former chief clerk (in which role he recruited William Farrer in 1898 to get his wheat expertise) and then chief inspector of agriculture in New South Wales, into service to examine the prospects of its new possession. Campbell found that, for all the talk of several decades, the South Australian government had in reality done very little to encourage pastoral, and even less to encourage agricultural, development of the north. The one major experiment had been carried out with private money: in 1890 an individual had invested a considerable sum of money to establish a tobacco plantation. Thirty hectares had been cleared and stumped, and a tobacco curing shed erected. The first crop had brought ten and ninepence a pound on the Dresden market, but the experiment was abandoned when the owner's father died.

Campbell was concerned that urgent experimental work was not being done. He reported that nothing was known about particular needs in the Territory in the areas of sowing and preparation. He recommended that the cleared land on the abandoned tobacco plantation be sown in fodder, cereals and fruit; that the area along the Daly River be investigated as being possibly suitable for grassland on which to run domesticated buffalo; that sheep be raised around Katherine to find whether an industry could be based there, and that experiments be undertaken to find whether cigar leaf tobacco could be cultivated in the Territory on an economic basis.

Nothing much came of Campbell's recommendations. Twenty-five years later the Chinese involved in rice-growing found that it was more profitable to open a commercial business in the towns; the peanuts grown at Katherine and near the Daly River were a failure; the cattle by and large on the big properties were of inferior quality and many ran wild.

It was not that the federal government had not tried to do something. The Fisher Labor government, which was in power in Melbourne when South Australia finally relinquished control of the Northern Territory, intended that the land monopolists be controlled, and that pastoral holdings be limited in size. But — as so often happens — the intentions of the political masters were well and truly thwarted by the civil servants appointed to implement the policy. The first administrator was a ruthlessly reactionary and censorious Scot, John Anderson Gilruth. He had no sympathy for the government's policy of breaking up the large pastoral holdings and the Fisher government left office with its plans for the Territory in tatters. In addition, the largest meat-producing company in the world, Vestey Brothers, was invited by Gilruth to take up holdings in the Territory. He dismissed the heads of the departments in Darwin which administered land, Aboriginal affairs and agriculture. The frame of mind of the man is revealed by one of his last acts before being forced to resign: he abolished trial by jury except for murder and he rationed beer sales in the Northern Territory.

Vestey was not slow in taking up Gilruth's invitation and the company quickly acquired 36,000 square miles of property. The Vestey company was totally and effectively opposed to the railway being built north to Darwin, simply because it would increase political pressure to break up the large pastoral holdings to allow more intensive land use. The plans for a government-owned meatworks were subverted and in 1917 a Vestey meatworks started up (it lasted only three years, closing partly due to lack of shipping space out of Darwin, but the cattle raising operation continued). During the 1920s more properties were added to the English company's portfolio. But the performance of the properties was poor. In 1927 meat exports from the Northern Territory were lower than they had been at the turn of the century, and the depression of the 1930s exacerbated the Vestey situation.

In 1937 the Payne-Fletcher report, commissioned by the Lyons government, urged the restructuring of the large pastoral properties on the grounds that the leases were too large to be controlled by one management. The report was, not unexpectedly, anathema to the large pastoral companies — and it was not just Vestey in this category — which all held long leases without improvement or development conditions. War broke out before any of the report's recommendations could be implemented and it was not until 1949, under Chifley, that the Federal government in Canberra turned its attention to the question of the Northern Territory pastoral leases. A cabinet committee in that year recommended they be replaced by development leases with very specific improvement conditions.

Again, the Vestey interest came up trumps — the company got its long-term leases at a very low rent — and the reformers were thwarted. (Wave Hill, which covered three million acres, in later times, attracted an annual rent of just $17,000.) Chifley was defeated in 1949 and the new Liberal government under Robert Menzies followed its conservative antecedents and turned its attention away from the vast north. Most of the leases were due to expire in 1965; the Menzies government extended them to the year 2004. Although Vestey was only one of several companies involved with these pastoral leases, its size of operation and the spectacular secrecy with which it has always cloaked its activities tended to draw attention to it. By 1940 the Australian holdings of what by then had become Vestey group totalled 63,000 square miles.

It was always difficult to discover exactly what Vesteys owned and operated, but in 1980 Vestey it still controlled vast stations in the north: Waterloo and Mistake Creek on the Northern Territory-Western Australia border; Wave Hill in the Territory; Nutwood Downs east of Daly Waters; Morestone Downs on the Northern Territory-Queensland border; Coolulah near Mount Isa; Doonemabullah near Jericho; Fitzroy Vale, Lake Learnouth, Oban and Archer all near Rockhampton. It also had large interests in meatworks and butchers' shops in Australia. (In 1992, as part of an international liquidation of Vestey interests, six stations were sold at auction for a total of $38 million and others were subsequently unloaded in separate deals.)

Life was never easy for the outback men employed on the Vestey cattle stations. Their wages were reputed to be less generous than other station operators. This can be partly explained by the parlous financial state the stations were in for much of the 1920s and 1930s. While the paternalism of Vestey as an employer meant that workers were rarely fired or wanted for food after they retired, it also meant that strict rules were applied which did not sit well with the stockmen. Liquor was banned in a part of the world which had one of the highest alcohol consumptions per head of population. In 1966 Aboriginal workers walked off Wave Hill in protest at the fact that they were paid lower wages that white employees.

Of course, it is a matter for argument whether the course of pastoral and agricultural development would have been any different in the north had different policies been pursued. On the one hand, it has been said that Menzies' action in the early 1950s ensured that the Territory was locked up for half a century. It seemed certain that the decision by the Hawke Labor government in Canberra to abandon the proposed Alice Springs-Darwin railway in the 1980s would put off again the prospect of more intensive use of this vast tract of land. The pastoral and agricultural hopes, one view would have it, had suffered death by a thousand indecisions.

Yet, even if the railway had been built earlier than it was, and had the leases had been terminated much earlier than they were — or at least subjected to improvement conditions — would things have been much different? Even if Campbell's experimental farms had been able to raise sheep and grow tobacco, would there ever have been processing plants or markets? Only now things are beginning to change. In 2012, the Northern Territory authorities published an extensive manual on growing vegetables in the tropics. As of 2011, cattle still accounted for 53.5 per cent of the primary sector output in the Territory. But then horticulture had grown to a 26 per cent share: mangoes were produced to the value of $80 million, and there were table grapes, bananas and melons.

But, in historical terms, populating (and cultivating) the north, has been a succession of disappointments and setbacks.

In Western Australia, as will be seen later, the authorities had to go to extraordinary lengths to attract people to take up land, and most of the areas being offered were a great deal more attractive than anything the north had to offer. White men believed it to be unhealthy to toil in the canefields of Queensland. The white settlers simply did not like the idea of trying to farm in the tropics. Nor did sheep take to the north: their numbers in the Territory declined from 107,000 to just 6,000 between 1888 and 1921. The real problem was that the north could never be developed cheaply, and Australia could compete on the world market only when it could produce goods cheaply as in the case of letting sheep roam over thousands of acres with minimum supervision, or cutting vast acreages of wheat with modern machinery. Much of Australia's rural production was nurtured and sustained by means of tariff protection and subsidy.

Neither of those is politically realistic today.

Burrawang West station in central New South Wales is still a working farm (mainly cattle these days) and is also billed as a luxury five-star retreat. But from the 1880s it was wall-to-wall sheep, some 273,000 at a time. This shows the interior of the shearing shed as sorting and classing of the wool gets under way.

National Library of Australia

Chapter 7
All that Glisters is not Gold

Winnowing peas was a hot and grubby task, and one that involved the whole family as this 1915 photograph shows.

J.S. Battye Library 2951B/46

THE PROMOTERS OF Western Australia had more to work with than the advocates of the north, even though it was hard getting going. While the introduction of convicts to Western Australia did provide the economic development trigger that had been so desperately needed, transportation did not prevent the colony's economic growth distorted. There was little growth of agriculture in the years of transportation: between 1850 and 1853 the area sown in crops expanded only from 7,419 acres to 10,299 acres. It was easier and more profitable to rear sheep for wool and mutton, a temptation that was to lead to Western Australia being a net importer of food for several years.

The little cropping that was done was rarely systematic. A typical set-up would be a few acres of wheat next door to several acres of barley. The seed was sown broadcast and then bullock teams would pull harrows across the field. In the first two decades of agriculture in the west the crops were cut by scythe, with the sheaves left in the fields to dry. The grain was spread on hard ground and trodden out from the straw, the latter being kept for the stables, thatching or chaff.

A picture of the farming year in that early era was left by three brothers who ran a property near York, William, Samuel and Lockier Burges. The diary began in early April. Then the farmers were busy ploughing, using both horse and bullocks, that work interspersed with mending the roof of house and barn for the winter, and brewing beer. When the rains came, the brothers were back in the fields sowing, first barley, then wheat, and that was followed into June by more sowing of grain and hay.

The month of July was spent tending the kitchen garden and orchard and carrying out repairs on the property and buildings. August included the digging of potatoes which had been planted in the autumn.

After the sheep had been brought in and washed, shearing occupied the first part of October, and then followed the washing and packing of the wool. While the last of the shearing was under way, the brothers were out in the fields cutting the hay, and then the fields were ploughed for fallow. Hardly had that been finished than it was time to reap the barley, and on 27 November harvesting of the wheat began, a task which took nearly a month. Meanwhile the wool clip was on a dray being pulled by eight bullocks on the way to Perth to be sold.

January and early February were spent treading out the barley and wheat. In March the brothers took a holiday in Perth, after which they would be ready for another busy year as the cycle started once again in April.

These brothers were clearly familiar with farming methods, but that could not be said for the majority of Western Australia's early agriculturalists. By the 1870s general ignorance of farming methods had led to soil exhaustion over significant areas, so that the land was yielding poor crops even in good seasons.

An even more devastating blow to agriculture in the colony was a combination, in the early years of the 1870s, of an extended drought and a blight of red rust on wheat. Fields which had been sown and harvested for many years were suddenly abandoned, and some of the smaller rural settlements became ghost villages. In 1872 another strike of red rust hit several districts, and by 1873 nearly 6,000 acres had gone out of production, followed by another 2,000 acres the following year. Western Australia was thus firmly established as an importer of flour and grain. The shortage of agricultural products was complicated by the gold rush in the west which lasted from 1892 until 1907, during which large quantities of food had to be imported from the east of Australia. (It must be added, however, that gold saved Western Australia's bacon in the 1890s, the colony prospering while its eastern counterparts suffered through depression and drought; and the farmers of the colony also did well with good prices for their produce.

Western Australia's growth had been static for forty years when, in 1887, an agricultural commission was appointed to find ways to break this rural stagnation. It met at a time when there had been no increase in cropping for fifteen years. One of the problems which had beset the pastoral and agricultural communities was the system of barter, a system which had been imposed upon the country folk by the lack of enough money in circulation. Merchants issued their own pound notes in the absence of the real thing, and these were passed from hand to hand. More common, though, were promissory notes (known as 'shinplasters'), and even the tails of wild dogs became accepted as worth ten shillings and were passed as payment. Boat owners who transported people along the Western Australian coast would find that they possessed orders made out on storekeepers all over the colony instead of cash payment for fares, and it would take them months to extract cash from these. Many farmers never touched coin of the realm — the storekeeper who paid all their bills (including that for the doctor) would provide the goods they needed, and even grind their wheat, all of which would be deducted from the proceeds of their crop. It was a form of subsistence farming that was more usually found in primitive societies. The great drawback to the system was that it did not encourage the farmer to expand his output because there was never any cash incentive for so doing. It was a slow, backward and, to the outside world, practically unknown community. Western Australia was fortunate to get as its first premier Sir John Forrest, who realised that gold alone was not the basis of future prosperity. It was land settlement.

Over the decade before federation the Western Australian government passed a series of acts which were designed to get people on to the land as quickly as possible. It was largely the work of Forrest, who held the positions of premier and treasurer for the decade and through until February 1901.

First, land in the south-western division of the colony was offered at ten shillings an acre, to be paid in twenty annual instalments of sixpence an acre (provided improvements were made, a condition in all subsequent legislation). Land in the Kimberley region was made available at half the previous lease rental provided it was stocked with either ten sheep or one cattle beast for every 1,000 acres. The Midland Railway Company was given 12,000 acres of land for every mile of line laid, and then land grants were made to the Western Australian Land Company which laid the railway between Beverley and Albany on the south coast. The Midland company was floated in London in 1890 and laid 277 miles (445km) of track from a Midland Junction near Perth to Walkaway, where it linked with an isolated section of government railway running south from Geraldton. The bulk of the company's revenue over its long life — it was bought out by the state government in 1964 — derived from its haulage of agricultural products.

Four years before the Midland float, the West Australian government concluded a deal with an English syndicate, the Western Australian Land Company. (This took over from the company from Sir Anthony Horden, the Sydney retailer, who had founded the land company but died aboard ship on his return to Australia in 1886.) It was also structured on the land-grant principle. The company — which was better known as the Great Southern Railway — agreed to build a line between Beverley and Albany, a distance of 242 miles (389km). Albany was the colony's main deepwater port until Fremantle was developed, and it took five days to get to Albany by coach from Perth. The company was to get 12,000 acres for each mile of railway completed. The company was also contracted to bring 5,000 immigrants from the United Kingdom to populate and farm the lands along the route. However, the company could not find enough people wanting to lease all this land it was being granted so in 1896 the government bought it out for £1.1 million.

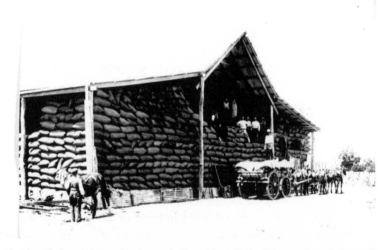

In the days before wheat silos located alongside railway lines, grain was bagged and then manhandled into stacks like this. Not only did it involve back-breaking work but the bags were a temptation to vermin, especially when stacked in piles in the open in railway yards.

J.S. Battye Library 9399P

Other measures taken by the Forrest administration included a duty of the fourpence a bushel was levied on imported wheat to make it more attractive for Australians to grow the grain. The Homestead Act provided that any head of a family or male over eighteen years of age could, provided they already owned less than 100 acres, pay £1 and be given 160 acres which, if they improved the land and farmed for seven years, would be theirs. The rent relief to the squatters was accompanied by provision for twenty-acre blocks of land for working men — they paid £2 an acre, the amount due over twenty years, the idea being that the colony would become self-sufficient in food if town and other workers were encouraged to devote their spare time to these allotments. Land covered in poisonous plants (known as 'poison land') was sold at one and threepence an acre, payable over thirty years. The government also purchased large estates bounding the new railway lines it was pushing out at breakneck speed, and these estates were then broken up into small selections. An Act of 1894 established the Agricultural Bank which lent money against improvements. When new land was taken up, the government paid half the cost of the survey. By 1898 land was available on conditional purchase with terms so easy as to be within the reach of anyone prepared to take up selections and develop them.

It was the beginning of a transformation. Not only had wheat and other crop production been retarded over a number of years, but dairying had been a depressed industry because there was little market and even less labour available — even by 1914 butter production was low and cheese production almost non-existent. In 1896 there was only 2,393 acres of orchard land (in 1848 there had been so little orchard land that it was not worth counting).

The Agricultural Bank, and its growing role, was the crucial factor. Loan money was needed for agriculture: if you were going to grow wheat on a viable basis you had to sow 200 acres, and that needed finance. By 1906 the Bank could lend on the full value of improvements.

At federation, mining, timber and the pastoral industries were the mainstay of the Western Australian economy and, while it was soon to expand, agriculture was of minor importance. Between 1891 and 1900 the colony's population increased from 53,279 to 179,708 (largely as a result of the gold discoveries). More significantly the area of land under crops grew from 64,210 to 201,338 acres (in 1949 it was 4,292,730 acres).

But it wasn't enough. In 1900 Western Australia imported nearly five million pounds of butter, nearly one million pounds of cheese, 94,898 cases of preserved milk, more than three million pounds of bacon and ham, 770 tons of oatmeal and 610,643 bushels of wheat. Even by 1905 the state's agricultural imports cost more than £1 million in cash and there were still 30 million acres of land vacant in the regular rainfall belt.

It was the downturn in gold mining which inadvertently gave Western Australia a new impetus in farming. This was made possible by the foresight of those politicians who had provided the legal and financial skeleton. Gold production fell off noticeably between 1905 and 1908. The result was pronounced unemployment on the goldfields, on the wharves, in the public service and throughout the state. When gold mining had declined in other colonies the immediate result had been large-scale emigration.

Fortunately for Western Australia it had the man to meet the challenge of the times, James Mitchell, who became Minister for Agriculture and Lands in 1909. A former lawyer from the town of Northam, Mitchell was not a man to tolerate opposition when he had made up his mind. He had set his sights on the millions of acres north of Geraldton, inland from Ajana. He changed the system of survey before selection to selection before survey, hired every private surveyor in Western Australia and took on men who needed to be trained. The next thing was to find the farmers for these hundreds of 1,000-acre blocks. Mitchell found them on the goldfields. They were mainly men without agricultural experience and, because they were unemployed, had little or no money to their names. Moreover as far as the minister was concerned here was a group of men with idle hands.

Long before implement salesmen produced their glossy brochures and easy terms, the West Australian farmer would make do with his home-made equipment. Typical was this roller for clearing scrubland. This photograph was taken about 1913.

J.S. Battye Library 595B/8

Once more the Agricultural Bank was the source of bounty. It was now permitted to lend all the cost of clearing land, and the amount available for loan was shown on the plan of each block in advance of its being offered for sale. The men taking up the land knew that the day they stepped on to a block they would have money in their pocket, and they knew exactly how much it would be. George Sutton came to Western Australia at this time. A former assistant of William Farrer, he had been appointed Commissioner for the Wheatbelt and later became the state's director of agriculture. He visited the Yorkrakine settlement soon after his arrival. Here fifty men had each been given 1,000 acres and £50 to get started. Sutton wrote:

> Imagine my repercussions to this venture when I tell you that in New South Wales in the previous year, a young acquaintance of mine with £500 capital, a skilled horseman with a life-long experience of draught horses and two years' experience on a wheat farm cropping 3,000 acres annually, had been refused a block of land by the New South Wales Land Board because it was considered that he had neither enough capital nor sufficient experience to operate his own wheat farm successfully.

However, by 1911 the settlers at Yorkrakine, most of whom had been taken from among the unemployed at Fremantle, had cleared about a fifth of the land and had on average 200 acres under crop. Although Sutton decried the creation of what he called 'the Agricultural Bank psychology', which condition was typified by a settler failing to understand that eventually all the money had to be paid back, he agreed nevertheless that the end result of Mitchell's policy was spectacular. (Not everyone at the time saw it in quite such glowing terms: the bad rainfall years between 1911 and 1914 saw many of the new farmers in difficulty and Mitchell was accorded the blame for what was called over-optimism. However, Mitchell did not lose his enthusiasm for settlement schemes, as he would show after World War I.)

In 1906 the state had exported £7 worth of wheat; in 1928 the export value of wheat was £7 million. The Coolgardie water scheme which brought in new lands in the Avon Valley and Midland districts resulted in a thirty-three-fold increase in agricultural production in twenty-seven years. In 1900 Western Australia produced 774,000 bushels of wheat, and in 1915-16 the harvest was 18,236,000 bushels, of which 14 million were exported.

At the turn of the century, the rate of land alienation in Western Australia, Queensland and New South Wales was roughly equal. In Queensland in 1901 the acreage alienated was 365,000; in New South Wales 361,000, and in

Western Australia the figure was 352,000. Between 1904 and 1908 the annual
average figures were:

Queensland	790,000 acres
New South Wales	360,000
Western Australia	1,080,000

While the number of new settlers in the other two states rose marginally,
Western Australia by 1908 was putting 4,700 people a year on the land
compared with 1,888 in 1901.

Forrest had foreseen that gold, while it gave Western Australia the economic
take-off that it desperately needed, was no long-term financial base. Had he
and Mitchell not taken the action they did, the end of the gold might have
plunged the state into an economic crisis and brought it close to collapse. After
all, without the gold it would have had no alternative employment for the
miners, nor the money to pay for imported food. As it was, the farmer was
Western Australia's saviour.

**Picking raspberries in Victoria in 1905. Labour-intensive farming was fine so long as wages
were pitifully small.**

National Library of Australia

Chapter 8
One Good Crop Every Ten Years

Cutting and carting hay in southern Tasmania in 1939, where horses were still an important part of farm operations. Stockpiles of hay always came in handing in times of drought and seasonal shortages; on the mainland, such times saw huge consignments moved over the railways systems.

National Library of Australia

A USTRALIAN POLITICIANS, IT seemed, never learned from past mistakes when it came to farming and land development. The miseries of selection where blocks were too small and the land too poor, the sharp lesson of the disasters which had befallen wheat growers who ignored the Goyder line — neither had prevented the same mistakes being made again, as witness the conclusion of the South Australian inquiry into pastoral and marginal lands, delivered in
1947:

A considerable part of the new farming of 1920-30 had been based on the assumption that farming is easy ... that hard work alone will enable a farmer to succeed. Wheat farming had been developed in districts which were too uncertain in their rainfall. Dairy farms had been established which were too small to enable a man to earn his living.

In 1929 Mr Justice Pike. reporting to the federal government on losses on the soldier settlement schemes after World War I, attributed all the problems to the settlers having too little capital, not enough land to support themselves and not enough experience. Justice Pike noted:

There seems to be a general impression that anyone can make a farmer, but in these days of keen competition a farmer has to be a man of many parts, particularly having regard to the uncertain climatic conditions of Australia.

Not that the millions of acres of Australia's agricultural and pastoral lands were all in the hands of impoverished amateurs grasping at some elusive vision of Arcadian bliss, but — a point made in the previous chapter — the continent is not one of the better farming prospects in the world. Farming in most of its guises was sustained for a considerable length of time in Australia only by artificial means, whether it be bounty on sugar, guaranteed prices, tariffs on imported agricultural produce, or one of the myriad of devices which successive governments, federal and colonial, have used to protect the Australian farmer from the all too chill winds of foreign competition. In 1985 television viewers across the country watched as Victorian dairy farmers raided local supermarkets as a protest against the importation of subsidised Scandinavian and New Zealand cheeses — all of them cheaper in delivery costs than the local product. There was never, as far as one could see, a moment's reflection on the fact that these Victorian farmers could not compete on the open market. The farming journals of

1985 reflected the same cheerful indifference to the realities of free trade as farming organisations exerted much effort to maintain and increase the protection and public money which was employed to save the farmers from collapse. Yet, 27 years later, one can little imagine the farmers being able to command the headlines in such a way, so rapid has been the emergence of another more powerful pillar of the economy in the mining and energy section.

Could it still be said, as the first edition of this work maintained in 1986, that "the Australian economy would, without question, itself collapse without the massive amounts of money earned by export of primary produce"? Well, of course, we could not soldier on without either the food to feed ourselves nor the export earnings from what is exported on our behalves. But one would probably no longer express it in such apocalyptic terms.

Farming is still vital. It's just probable that fewer people today realise the fact, even compared with 1986.

As the National Farmers' Federation points out, every Australian farmer produces enough to feed 600 people (150 domestically and 450 overseas). Yet — and here's fact that shows how this economy has changed — the agriculture sector contributes just three per cent of Australia's gross domestic product. That's at the farm gate; add in the processing and you get to 12 per cent. But farming is vital to the national wellbeing, bringing in around $35 billion a year in foreign earnings.

But has it got any easier for the man and woman on the land. In some ways, yes: the isolation has gone, thanks to good roads that allow daily newspaper delivery and shopping trips to supermarkets in town, radio and satellite television. But the nature of this land continues to be a challenge: the good crops come more often, but there are still plenty of bad years.

Land selection in Tasmania

To the casual observer, Tasmania would seem to be one of the choicer patches: it has no deserts or arid zones, and its temperate climate with good annual rainfall would suggest a land of plenty. But the reality for more than 100 years was quite the opposite.

Tasmania had been the country's main wheat producer between 1820 and 1850, but this output partially replaced over the years as some land was converted to growing barley and oats. Merinos were introduced early in Tasmania's history, but the climate favoured more the Polwarth and Corriedale breeds, and eventually the island's farmers evolved the Cormo, a sheep which is suited to the local conditions and produces fine wool. Tasmania's became the most diversified of the agricultural economies in Australia. Its butter and cheese from across Bass Strait became popular on the mainland. It was in fruit — apples, pears, red and black currants, strawberries and raspberries — that the island farmers excelled. The climate of Tasmania allowed landholders to diversify almost at will.

A good example of a diversified property was Panshanger, south of Longford. A writer from the *Melbourne Leader* who visited the property in 1875 said that good apples, pears and plums were produced and that cherries grew everywhere.

The apples were crushed in the mill in the garden and produced cider for the hands hired at shearing and harvest times. There was a kitchen garden of five acres which produced a range of vegetables for the house. The run was 6,560 acres, and 200 acres were put aside for grain and hay cultivation. Paddocks were sown in perennial rye-grass, white clover or prolific cocksfoot. The squatter, Joseph Archer, ran 11,500 sheep and 300 cattle, mainly Herefords.

One of the underlying reasons for Tasmania's problems was the unwillingness of the colony's government to tighten land development laws as had been done on the mainland. By the time of federation, selection grants carried no requirement for improvements (a first step in that direction was taken in 1903) and dummying was rampant. In 1910 a royal commission found that there was no chance of obtaining a conviction when only two people were involved. As had been the case fifty years before across Bass Strait, the existing landowners acquired more land simply by having agents or 'dummies' obtain the selection, the ownership being transferred later. The commission, illustrating the blatant nature of the business, cited an instance where a landowner and his agent applied for thirteen land transfers at the one time.

Nor had the government provided the infrastructure. The pace of railway development was well behind that of the mainland, and there was never any intention of bringing every farmer within fifteen miles of a railway. While such a policy proved in the long term in the mainland states to be profligate, the extravagant railway networks there did at least provide the main impetus for development of new lands. But the Tasmanians never bothered in many instances to build even roads before opening up an area for selection. There was a particularly serious lack of railways or roads in the north of the island, and some dairy farmers well into the twentieth century found the only way to get their milk to market was to transport it over rough tracks on sleighs.

Many of the selections were on third-class land, quite suited to pastoralism but inadequate for a small holding to be economically viable. Between 1903 and 1911 the area of pastoral land in Tasmania declined from 264,417 acres to 149,328 acres. The land lost to pastoralism was, for the most part, left idle once it had been cut up into selections.

As will be seen, Tasmanian farming was also typified (except in dairying) by low production, soil depletion and lagging mechanisation. However, none of these was mentioned in a Tasmanian government publication of 1928, designed to lure migrants from Britain.

Backbreaking work was involved in harvesting potatoes, as seen here in Western Australia.

National Library of Australia

The figures produced in that publication show just how heavily dependent the island state was on cropping: 100,000 acres were sown in grain crops, 40,000 acres in root (mainly potato) crops; hay and green fodder covered another 100,000 acres, with orchards totalling 35,000 acres in area. Potato cropping was expanding, particularly as part of the policy of closer settlement, and most of these farms were less than 100 acres in area. Of the orchard land, nearly three-quarters was in apple production. Setting up an apple orchard was quite an expensive business, the following being the first year's costs:

15 acres	Pounds/shillings/pence
1500 trees	£75/0/0
Land at £5 acre	£75/0/0
Clearing at £15 acre	£225/0/0
Ploughing at £1/10/0 acre	£22/10/0
Disking at 6/acre	£4/10/0
Fencing	£120/0/0

15 acres	Pounds/shillings/pence (Continued)
Manure	£15/0/0
Planting	£22/10/0
Total	£559/10/0

That was for just the first year, and the trees did not reach bearing stage until the seventh year. The writer of this official booklet did state that many orchards in Tasmania had been seriously affected and stunted in growth by the trees being allowed to bear heavy crops in their younger years. Since 1884, when 100 cases had been chilled and shipped to Britain aboard the *SS Warwick* Tasmanian growers had found a lucrative export market, and in 1928 shipped 1.5 million bushels of apples.

It should have been a lot more. An economic study of Tasmanian farming published in 1929 revealed that a Tasmanian worker produced, on average, £330 worth of crops, compared with an average of £502 from a mainland farm worker. It was the large-scale wheat growing on the mainland of Australia, not possible in Tasmania, which accounted for some of the difference. The average for Tasmania was one farm worker per 41 acres whereas the average acreage per worker was 160 in the rest of the nation. The flat land and the greater use of machinery made all the difference, Tasmanian wheat-growing being retarded through lack of capital and shortage of flat land. Yet even compared with Queensland, where cropping was more likely to be labour-intensive cane-growing, the Tasmanians lagged in value of production in 1927 when these figures were taken. Queensland was able to be ahead on value of production per person even when it needed a worker for every 29 acres against Tasmania's 41.

The real problem was that of soil robbery, through both lack of fertiliser and through repetition of cash crops which did little to restore natural fertility. While the area sown in potatoes between 1890 and the time of the study (1929) had grown substantially, it had been paralleled by steadily diminishing yield, not only by reason of soil exhaustion but also the widespread habit of planting diseased seed potatoes. The result was that potato production over forty years had, per acre, been halved. The awareness of the need both to raise crops which helped restore fertility (such as seed clover) and to have mixed farming with the animals producing natural fertiliser had been lost on many of the state's agriculturalists.

In dairying, the Tasmanian was producing more per person than his mainland counterpart, the island's climate being highly favourable to this type of primary production. Moreover the survey showed that Tasmania's dairy production could have been a great deal higher than it was.

Breeding was poor, and the majority of herds were made up of scrubs. Tasmanian dairy factories were spending twice as much to manufacture a pound of butter as the factories in other states. The clincher was the production of butter-fat per acre, which revealed the quality of output: on fifty farms surveyed in New Zealand, they produced 125 pounds weight of butter-fat per acre; on five farms surveyed in Tasmania in 1926-7 the average was 30 pounds weight — or one sixth! However, Tasmanian farmers did have the Paterson Scheme, which subsidised the export payment for butter so that the New Zealand and Tasmanian farmers were earning roughly the same amount.

Tasmanian wheat production stagnated in the mid-nineteenth century like that on the mainland, but when mainland wheat production got under way again as railways made it possible to bring more and more land into use, Tasmania was left behind. It was ironic, considering that in the 1820s Tasmanian wheat production had exceeded that of New South Wales.

The struggle to grow wheat

Throughout Australia the early story of wheat was not one of inspiring success. In 1851 New South Wales still had to import 140,000 bushels of wheat and 8.3 million pounds of flour; in 1853, as the population was expanding, the imports amounted to 248,816 bushels and 25 million respectively. With the scarcity of labour, it was actually cheaper to import wheat than grow it in New South Wales. Anyway, it was possible to make larger profits with sheep and cattle. The pastoralist could very easily turn his stock on to unalienated Crown land for a period, and not be troubled for doing so, but it was not as easy to plough and sow land that was not yours. As usual, the pastoralist in early Australia seemed to have all the right cards in his hand.

But even if the settler did want to grow wheat, unless he was close to a major town, there was the annual headache of how to get the produce to market. Roads, where they existed, were poor and wheat could not be on the road for a month or two without suffering in quality. River transport was not much better in the days of sail — in Tasmania the boats which took the wheat from Pittwater down river to Hobart forty miles away could take up to two weeks to cover the distance. Before the construction wave during the railway development age, wheat cultivation in New South Wales actually decreased in some seasons, such as that of 1857 and 89,195 acres were planted in the crop compared with 106,124 acres the previous season.

The impact of railway development was significant. In 1890, by which time most major lines and many of the branches were built, wheat acreage in New South Wales was 419,789. In 1901 it was 1.4 million acres. At the turn of the century the new varieties of wheat, including those developed by William Farrer, and the increased use of super phosphates, had made wheat growing much more productive and profitable.

The one colony which had shown a great interest in wheat from the start was South Australia. By 1865 the farmers there had planted 600,000 acres in wheat. In was not until 1890 that Victoria overhauled its neighbour in wheat production, and New South Wales became the nation's leading producer only in 1923. The reason for South Australia's early leap forward was that Adelaide had large plains at its back door, and that land was easily accessible for the new settler. There was no mountain barrier which separated the grower from the city and ports, and the climate showed itself to be favourable to wheat growing.

South Australia's expansion had ceased during the droughts of the 1880s when those who, as detailed earlier in this book, had ignored the Goyder rainfall line suffered great loss and misery as the land dried up and their crops failed to grow. It was not until 1910 that wheat production once again increased, this time with the introduction of phosphate fertilisers. The farmers were hard to convince at the start; so great had been their hopes when they poured out into the Mallee scrub and the Yorke Peninsula, and so bitter were their disappointments of the past decades that they were reluctant to spend what little money they had left on something that might also turn out to be only an illusory promise of better things. But by the turn of the century nearly a quarter of South Australia's wheatlands was being dressed with superphosphate. The results were more marked in the higher rainfall areas, which had been the first settled, simply because the fertiliser's benefits were limited in the Mallee areas when there was not enough rain. The new state Department of Agriculture also carried out a campaign for better cultivation methods, including weed control and allowing land fallow time to recover before another crop was sown.

Not all the farmers listened, and the headaches multiplied with a new land boom. By 1902 a great deal of Murray Mallee land in South Australia (roughly the area bounded by Pinnaroo in the east and Murray Bridge in the west) had already been settled, and by 1905 the lessons of the Goyder line were being forgotten and blocks of Mallee land were being carved up and settled.

In 1910 nearly 180,000 acres of Mallee were put down in wheat. A new wave of railway building took place, but the politicians in Adelaide hedged their bets — they did not want to pour too much money into this newly settled region in case it resulted in another agricultural disaster. They built the line from

Tailem Bend to Pinnaroo to the much cheaper narrow gauge of 3 feet 6 inches (1,067mm) rather than the broad gauge of 5 feet 3 inches (1,600mm) which was the norm throughout the main-line system of South Australia. Money was also saved by minimising earthworks and leaving the lines with heavy grades for the locomotives to battle, and by using light rails. In its 1914 general report, the South Australian Parliamentary Standing Committee on Railways noted examples of how light rails on country lines might have meant cost savings in construction but handicapped the efficiency of the lines later. The Tailem Bend-Pinnaroo section had been opened for traffic in September 1906, the line being made with forty-pound second-hand rails and the sleepers just laid on the ground surface without any ballast. As a result, speeds on the line were slow and by 1914 this track was incapable of taking trains which included heavy goods, or produce or livestock traffic. Another of the lines built in this region, the Tailem Bend to Paringa line completed in 1913, had speed limits on part of the route of twenty miles an hour.

All seemed well in the Murray Mallee for a few years, but then the bubble burst. This time it was not the drought which ravaged the Mallee wheat growers who had crossed the Goyder line, but the collapse in prices after World War I (although a few poor weather seasons had not helped and the continuing exploitative farming had led to serious erosion with worsening run-off after the rain that did fall). The soldier settlers were badly hit by the price collapse, and many of them abandoned their new farms, but they were joined in the exodus by many other longer established people, too. There was so little wheat to be carried out that on one section of the Peebinga railway line there were no trains at all. The winds blew away the topsoil and deposited sand in its place, and salting was a growing problem in those areas closer to the Murray River. Those farmers who stayed were given financial assistance, but then the depression of the 1930s struck.

It is arguable whether these farms would have survived had there been no depression. On ten occasions in twenty-six years the average yields on the Murray marginal lands were below five bushels an acre. Between 1933 and 1946 the population of the Murray Mallee fell by thirty-four per cent. A parliamentary committee set up to investigate the question of marginal land (mentioned at the opening of the chapter) based its conclusions on the inadequate size of properties, and drew attention to the too frequent cropping of marginal lands.

Such was the variation in the quality of land that the cost of producing a bushel of wheat in South Australia had varied from four and ninepence in the best areas to fifteen shillings and sevenpence in the worst, and the greater part of the South Australian wheat crop until 1935 was being produced at a loss. In 1935 the former South Australian Director of Agriculture, Arthur Perkins, stated that:

> ...practically all the land in South Australia open for settlement in the last thirty years had been Mallee scrub and that all the heavy work of clearing the land and bringing it into cultivation had been done by the individual farmers, mainly men of small capital."

For all their work, these men were lucky to get a good crop once in seven or ten years.

The men who settled the Mallee and Wimmera districts across the border in Victoria had a rough battle, too. The Wimmera had been settled by 1876, but then the rabbit reached plague proportions within a year or two. The settlement on the Mallee had been halted by the depression of the early 1890s, followed by the long drought, so that it was not until 1914 that this region was more closely settled.

Then came the war — and, for the farmer, an all too brief period of prosperity.

Chapter 9
A Million Farmers on a Million Farms

Everyone hung on the prices at the wool sales, the farmers and their wives getting dressed up for the trip to town. This was taken before the start of a sale in Goulburn, New South Wales, in November 1933.

National Library of Australia

A FEW DAYS BEFORE war was declared in 1914, the Sydney wool sale was cancelled at short notice. Most European buyers had cancelled their purchase instructions, and it looked as if there would not be enough ships to carry the clip to Europe with the British about to charter a large part of the merchant fleet for war duty. The pastoralists were told not to send any more wool to the stores.

While the wool was soon to be sorely and urgently needed, there remained throughout the war a problem with finding enough ships, and there were to be some tight moments later in the conflict when Britain tried to withdraw ships after Australia had gone out on a limb to produce record amounts of primary produce for the mother country. Within a few weeks of the outbreak of World War I, the Queensland parliament passed the Queensland Meat Supply for Imperial Uses Act (followed in 1915 by similar legislation in New South Wales) a measure which forbade the export of meat from the state to any purchaser other than the British government once the authorities in Brisbane invoked the act. The problem was that the drought of 1914 had created shortages of primary products in Australia, which meant that much of the Queensland meat was needed for the home market. With British permission, meat was also shipped to India and South Africa, and also to the French and Italian army authorities. By February 1915 the Imperial government in London took up the Queensland offer, the meat being needed to feed the armies on the western front, and all other sale contracts were cancelled from Brisbane.

Meanwhile, the wool salerooms had resumed their auctions. At the sale on 14 November 1914 prices lifted sharply, with the British buying heavily. Ten days later an embargo was placed on export of wool to anywhere other than Britain, or wherever London directed. The War Office in London was interested mainly in crossbred wool, which was the most suitable for uniforms. This left Australia with a large quantity of merino wool on its hands, and it was only after strenuous persuasion that the British took some of it. Then Japan and Imperial Russia obtained British permission to buy Australian wool. The result was record sales, all the wool from the previous season being sold by June 1915. Just before the war the Australian, British, South African and New Zealand governments had entered into an agreement which provided that surplus wool would be bought in and stored — an early form of price maintenance.

At the same time, the woolgrowers were not happy with the fact that limitations had been placed on the market, especially now that the situation had been transformed and wool was in acute demand. The Americans were particularly keen to pay good prices for the Australian product. London bowed to pressure from its southern dominions, and in 1916 agreed to buy the entire Australian and New Zealand wool clips for the duration of the war at 55 per cent above pre-war values. The sheep farmer had made a fortune.

When the war began there was no equivalent surplus of wheat. In fact the 1914 drought had ruined much of the crop, and Australia that year exported only a tenth of its normal consignments of wheat, and at one stage was importing wheat to meet the needs of the home market. Appeals were made to the farmers to increase the area under wheat; the people on the land responded and planted 12 million acres, which in turn yielded a record harvest of 179 million bushels. The problem was that there were not enough ships to carry this bounty to where it was desperately needed.

Two companies, Elder Smith and Antony Gibbs, were instructed by the Hughes administration to charter ships. But the British War Office was desperately short of bottoms: the western front in France required a vast fleet of ships to carry materiel and men across the English Channel, and there were the fronts at Gallipoli and then Salonika to be supplied. In fact, London told Prime Minister Billy Hughes that, rather than provide ships, they were actually going to have to requisition more Australian vessels for the war effort. They relented only when Hughes pointed out that the wheat farmers faced ruin if they could not ship the harvest which they had striven so hard to produce.

Yet by 1916 Australia had been able to get only half the tonnage it needed to move the wheat harvest. The problem was that, with German submarines in the Mediterranean Sea, colonial shipping was routed by way of the Cape of Good Hope, which added vital weeks to the journey. A ship could leave Liverpool and pick up a cargo of wheat from the eastern seaboard of North America and return in a third of the time it could make a return voyage to Australia. And then there were, the great wheat plains of Argentina, also much closer to the British market. The depredations of submarine warfare, which came close to halting the British War effort, made the British reluctant to send ships on long voyages to the other side of the world, and then they began diverting vessels from the Australian trade to the Atlantic routes. It was only in mid 1916 when it was thought that the U.S. wheat crop was going to be too small that more shipping was released to go to the Australian ports.

But the respite was only temporary for the Australian wheat growers. The American crop was larger than forecast, so again ships were sent to U.S. ports. The federal government had guaranteed an advance payment of an average of three shillings and threepence a bushel on wheat delivered to railway stations, a measure aimed at keeping the farmers' income at a reasonable level while the shipping problems were tackled.

The Royal Easter Show in Sydney these days is seen as a day out for city families with displays
of horses and other animals and vegetable-growing competitions, probably the only contact
with rural Australia most will have their in their lives. But at the 1917 show featured in this
photograph, it was much more a showcase for agricultural machinery and motor vehicles to
attract business from visiting farmers.

National Library of Australia

Hughes went to London and tried to fight for shipping to uplift the massive
Australian wheat crop. The British counter-offer was to purchase immediately
a large part of the stockpiled wheat on condition that Australia turned over to
London control of all its merchant shipping. Further, only ships registered in
Australian ports, including the government shipping line, could be used for the
wheat shipments. The British attitude was that once the wheat was theirs, there
would no longer be any pressure on them to actually ship it. The final deal was
for 3½ million tons, for which a good price was paid, Hughes being aware that
the wheat farmers would want to do as well out of the war as the woolgrowers
had done.

Only half a million tons had been collected by the time that wheat again
became available in the United States, and three million tons were left to rot
at railway sidings throughout Australia, much of it to be ruined by mice and
weevils. But at least the farmer had been paid.

In 1917 Britain purchased all the butter and cheese that Australia and New
Zealand could export. Fruit was declared non-essential, but the Allied armies

did need tinned food. The Australian fruit grower had never had a great deal of luck in persuading the British housewife to buy tinned jam or fruit before the war, but as production in Tasmania, Victoria and New South Wales swung into canning the fruit rather then shipping it chilled, there was not only a forty-fold increase in exports for the duration of the war, but an acceptance of the product afterwards, providing a continuing market for jam and tinned fruit. Other trades did well out of the war: hides were needed for boots and saddles and tallow for the glycerine that was used in cordite. By 1918 Britain's huge purchases from Australia had temporarily transformed the income of farmers in the latter. Wheat, which had sold in London in 1914 at five shillings a bushel, fetched over seventeen shillings immediately after the war. The wartime scarcities and high prices had been a great boon to Australian farming, and there was a widespread belief that the good times would last. The Australian farmer had an illusion of strength: the magazine *Australia Today* told its readers that 'the land can be cheaply worked, and the grain can be cheaply garnered'. Sir Joseph Carruthers, a former premier of New South Wales, was stumping the country with his campaign for bringing migrants from Britain to settle the land. 'A million farmers on a million farms' was the catchcry of his campaign.

Another former politician had also been busy. John Christian Watson, Australian Prime Minister in 1904, had been eager to be of public service during the war. One of his efforts was to circulate the troops serving overseas with a questionnaire, asking them what they wanted to do after the war. Of the 139,473 servicemen who bothered to reply, 35,680 wanted to settle on the land. Of those, only 21,000 had any farming experience. The survey was notable for the number of town and city dwellers who had, during the war, developed a hankering to try their hands at rural occupations.

An unhappy experiment

Soldier settlement was not a new concept. The Romans had settled much of their conquered territories with ex-soldiers, and just across the Tasman there had been a precedent set in New Zealand when, after the Land Wars, the British troopers had been given parcels of the land which had been confiscated from the defeated Maori tribes.

Australia did need more settlers, so the desire and the requirement came together. It was not a happy experiment. One of the problems with soldier settlement was that it was the one aspect of repatriation which was in the hands of the state governments simply because they controlled Crown land. The result was that there was no common standard for selection of settler, nor even of the quality of land. South Australia set a standard of farming instruction for the returned men, but other states were slow to follow. Meanwhile, the Commonwealth footed the bill to the tune of £1,000 per settler. The country, in the immediate post-war months, was suffused with emotional gratitude toward those who had served the cause of Empire, and the soldier settlement scheme caught the mood of the moment.

There was a more practical consideration: where were the jobs for all these men about to be released upon the employment market? At least placing them on a block of land would leave jobs for others. Added to the new wave of British migrants, there was a substantial class of new farmers, many of whom having only the faintest idea of what they were expected to achieve, and how. Much of the Crown land was carved up without the simplest of preliminaries such as soil surveys, as a result of which much of the land allocated was mediocre. Many blocks were also too small in area, and both land and improvements were charged at too high a price. The men were given thirty-two years to pay off their farms, and, had wartime prices for produce prevailed, there would have been no problem. Wheat farms were allocated in the Mallee, on the Darling Downs in Queensland and around Lake Cargelligo in New South Wales; soldiers became dairymen in Gippsland and the Western District of Victoria, at Dalby in Queensland and in north-western Tasmania; they were given land to grow sugar cane in Queensland; land was divided up for fruit growing in the Goulburn Valley, in the Murrum-bidgee Irrigation Area (particularly at Griffith) and in Tasmania's Tamar Valley.

Again, nothing had been learned from past experience. The endeavour to create a new class of small farmers was probably the most short-sighted, not to say stupid, aspect of the whole soldier settlement episode. Putting inexperienced people on the land had been tried before in Australia, and failed miserably. Failure was an inbuilt element of the whole scheme, and even if all the men had been hard working, skilled and practical farmers, they still could not have succeeded.

Not only was the land not good enough to sustain economic management, too often the stock was poor. The establishment of 37,561 soldier settlement farms after the war imposed a tremendous strain on livestock and plant supplies, so that dairy farmers were given cows of poor quality and fruit growers less than the best strains of fruit tree. Moreover, all this was purchased just after the war when the highest prices prevailed, and then prices fell dramatically. Even the cost of improvements was crippling, simply because skilled labour, in such short supply after the war, could be obtained only at highly inflated rates of payment.

In 1927 the federal government instructed a New South Wales judge, Mr Justice Pike, to inquire into the extent of losses of the soldier settlement scheme and how those losses should be apportioned between the states and the Commonwealth. Pike went further, and advanced his own explanation of why and how the scheme went sour.

He calculated the total loss to be £23,525,522. Seven million of that loss had been accounted for by the states lending to the settlers at a discount rate; in other words, the loans were being made at a rate of interest below that which the states themselves could borrow on the money market. Further expenses had been incurred because of the delay in purchase of land and the completion of surveys, roads and improvements, as a result of which interest-free periods had been granted to settlers. Dairy stock, said Pike, had been purchased at what he termed an 'entirely fictitious price', and there were men with war disabilities (such as gassing) who should never have been allowed to work a farm. He summed up by saying that the losses of the project could be attributed to the lack of capital on the part of the new farmers, the inadequate area of land most of them were given, the unsuitability to farming of many of the men, and the drop in prices. In the case of the latter, one example: butter had sold in Britain at 299 shillings and six pence in 1920; and was down to 169 shillings and six pence by 1926.

It was the load of debt which was as crippling as the fall in prices. Most of the soldier settlers had 100 per cent mortgages, and that mortgage price included the improvements which had been charged well above true value at the time. This debt situation made the situation hopeless from the outset.

An ordinary settler taking up land in New South Wales after the war would pay 1¼ per cent of the capital value in annual rental, or 2 per cent if he converted to conditional purchase. The soldier settler was paying a graduated interest which climbed from 3½ to 5½ or 6 per cent. So if a soldier settler and an ordinary settler owned adjoining blocks of the same size, the former would be sinking in a sea of debt while the latter probably managed to pay his way.

The states tried various ploys, such as remitting or writing down the debt, but the losses soon mounted again. More and more men walked off their properties as they realised that they could never produce enough to payoff their mounting debts. Judge Pike quoted the case of one New South Wales soldier settler who was, in the view of the Department of Agriculture, a capable and industrious farmer, yet after six years of remissions of debt still had outstanding accounts three times the value of his farm. Pike was of the opinion that had this man been allocated an economic parcel of land, and had he possessed some capital of his own, he could have been in a sound financial position.

By 1928 most of the settlers would have needed two or three harvests just to pay off their debts, but two-thirds of their assets belonged to creditors. Many had been sustained by the local storekeepers, but when it became apparent that the state governments had first call upon any security in the event of financial failure, the storekeepers reduced or withdrew their credit, and many demanded that the already desperate farmers should settle their accounts.

Pike found that men who had stuck it out had worked hard — the farms in the irrigation areas were well worked and well looked after, and in the Victorian Mallee many of the soldier settlers were attaining a higher return per acre than the other landowners. But the cards were stacked against them.

What followed was the Great Depression.

Chapter 10

Boiled Wheat and Treacle

A highlight in the life of many farming families (apart from local race meetings) was the local annual agricultural show. A group of local worthies pause in 1918 in the middle of a convivial luncheon long enough to have the local photographer record the occasion.

Wollongong Historical Society

FOR THOSE AGRICULTURALISTS and pastoralists who were not saddled with heavy debt, the mid twenties were a relatively prosperous time. For one thing, most of the established farmers had done quite well out of the war. Many of the wheat growers (although some were affected by drought in the latter part of the decade) had benefited from the good prices which held, in varying degrees, between 1915 and 1929.

Anyone writing about the Australian rural sector in 1925 would have concluded that the new era had arrived at last, and that the nation's farmers had encountered and overcome the worst in their struggle to establish a permanent agriculture. In the sugar fields, there had been a steady improvement in the quality of the canes grown, the methods of cultivation and the system of mechanical extraction in the mills, so that by 1924 the mills were getting a ton of sugar for every eight and a half tons of cane crushed, compared with ten tons just a few years previously. Most plantations had managed to sustain an output of two tons to the acre. At the then cost of production, someone with forty acres of cane would expect to make a profit of nearly £500. As mentioned earlier, there was at this time a world shortage of cotton, and the boll weevil, such a scourge in the American cotton fields, was unknown in Australia. So there was a heady optimism that millions of acres in Queensland would soon be covered with cotton plants.

One cheerful aspect of the primary scene was the development of minor crops, which lent much needed diversity to Australia's rural production. Broom millet grew well in areas of high rainfall, or in the irrigation areas, where the necessary intensive cultivation was possible. Being a summer crop, broom millet allowed the farmer to use the same land to grow potatoes and other crops for part of the year, so providing two incomes for the one piece of land. The millet fibre was finding a steady market both in Australia and abroad. Hops were found to flourish in deep loamy soils and in valleys where the hills protected the crop from high winds, and parts of Victoria and Tasmania had many areas which fitted this requirement. There was plenty of scope for development as hops were still being imported to meet the Australian demand in the brewing industry, and several thousands of dollars could be made by way of profit on medium-sized holdings. The only problem in this otherwise rosy picture was that hop growing was an expensive business to start, and it required about £70 an acre to get established.

The miseries of the Great Depression

Nevertheless, the Great Depression of 1929 hit Australia, and Australian farming, extremely hard. The country had brought much of the trouble on itself by heavy borrowing through some ill-judged public expenditure, followed by a fall in income through a collapse in the world prices for rural products and a decision to cease overseas borrowing because of the economic circumstances. The debt had risen during the previous decade partly owing to the borrowing for the soldier settlement schemes, and partly for the massive railway construction that had been undertaken in all states. Between 1919 and 1929 Australia's debt rose from £705 million to £1,117 million. In 1929 the interest alone was £28 million. What this meant was that when the crunch came, the federal and state governments had little room in which to manoeuvre: they could barely afford to pay what they owed, let alone borrow more to help the farmers weather the crisis.

There were other complicating factors. The weather had been bad in 1927-28, with a particularly vicious drought in South Australia and also a very dry season in Victoria and New South Wales. South Australia had more dry seasons in 1928-29 and 1929-30, and when the good harvest of 1930-31 came along prices throughout the world were the lowest in modern history. By the time the Wall Street crash occurred, South Australian wheat growers were already in an extremely precarious situation. Between 1928 and 1932 their indebtedness rose by 50 per cent.

Western Australia had experienced good wheat seasons, but the farmers there found themselves in a sticky position nonetheless. The reasons for this were fully revealed in the report later in the depression by the Western Australia Royal Commission on the Disabilities affecting Agriculture. This inquiry confirmed what many had suspected: that the lending to new farmers had been such as to extend an enormous blanket of debt across the state's agricultural and pastoral lands. On 30 April 1931 the Agricultural Bank was owed £14 million, including the money lent to soldier settlers. The private banks had not been slow to follow suit, either, so that in mid 1931 the total liabilities of Western Australia's 20,559 farmers involved in the wheat and sheep industries was a staggering £31 million and that did not include amounts owing to stock and station agents, private mortgagees, doctors and trades people. Land had been handed out so quickly that, of the alienated land in the state, 13 million acres was classed as improved but all of 22 million acres was still unimproved. In other words, for all the money handed out there was still much to be done to bring the land to its full productivity.

The commissioners were puzzled: since 1914, there had been a succession of good to moderate seasons and prices.

> Why, with such good seasons and prices, such an accumulation of indebtedness should have arisen is hard to say.

The royal commission found many reasons behind the plight of the farmers but the main ones were: the creation of a feeling and atmosphere of false prosperity by the excessive and over-easy borrowing; the unlimited extension of credit as merchants competed for the business especially since mechanical farming had come into existence; the readiness of stock and station companies to allow easy terms on implements; the mounting interest rates; a belief that high prices for wool and wheat would continue; the "more than forward policy' of the Agricultural Bank and the eagerness of the other banks to follow its lead, and the huge cost of the soldier settlement program. This Western Australian 'bubble' was summed up by the royal commission:

The whole industry was pyramided on good prices and lavish credit without due enquiry being made into production costs, world production of wheat and the value of the assets on which such credit was being extended. The government, through the Lands Department and the Agricultural Bank, together with all classes of the community ... are responsible for the accelerated and uneconomic development of the farming industry in Western Australia.

And, in another passage there was an even an exhortation to go back to four-legged motive power:

Your commissioners feel that tractor sellers are themselves responsible for their losses through bad debts in encouraging to buy tractors on terms which have been too extensive and liberal. They (the commissioners) are convinced that farmers will generally be wise to leave tractors alone, and those in possession of tractors will be well advised to gradually swing over to horses ... Your commissioners agree that the policy of refusing assistance for the purposes of power traction is the correct one.

By 1930 the depth of despair was so great in the western state that the Primary Producers' Association of Western Australia passed a motion calling on all members to cease production as a protest against the plight in which they now found themselves.

Throughout the country, farmers were evicted and country shopkeepers went broke. Many rural producers walked off their farms and moved to the cities to live on the dole. Those who stayed got used to the evening meal being boiled wheat and treacle, otherwise known as 'cocky's joy'.

The miseries of the Great Depression have been covered many times, but in Australia they have tended to concentrate on the unemployed of the cities. While these men and women were joined in their slums by thousands from the country, the majority of farmers tried to battle it out. The rigours of that fight against pressing debt and bankruptcy were charted in a book, *Life on the Land: what it means to-day*, published in 1932. Two women, Hilda Abbott and Gladys Owen, had travelled around the countryside recording their impressions. In northern New South Wales they set down in some detail the workings of a wheat farm. In the previous year the farmer's crop had brought him one and seven pence a bushel, and he was hoping that the government would provide a bounty. If that occurred, it would average his income per bushel over the two seasons to two shillings and sixpence.

At that rate it would require ten bushels of wheat an acre to pay his interest; four bushels for the fuel to keep his machinery running; one bushel each for bags, seed and superphosphate; almost two bushels for repairs and spare parts; and insurance on the crop, shire rates and transport of the crop to the railway would take almost another two bushels. In all, twenty-one bushels and acre were needed from land which normally produced twelve, an equation calculated to make even a Micawber horrified. Furthermore that calculation did not allow for depreciation or other costs such as food and clothing for his wife and children.

On a selection near Moree, they found that the family had to enclose the house with gauze to keep out plagues of mosquitoes, and that perishable foods were kept in a 'safe' fashioned with hessian which was kept wet. The previous year this man's wool had fetched nine pence a pound but his outgoings had been ten pence-halfpenny a pound. He was still on his land by dint of selling off part of his stock as fat lambs. The man's tasks, apart from tending to the sheep, included milking the cows that he had and separating milk and cream, preparing his horses for field work, cutting wood, and drawing and carting water to the house. These farmers were earning no money, so they had to make do with what they could produce on the land. Even when these travellers encountered a pastoralist who had no mortgage, they found that there was scant profit — three farthings per pound, in fact.

By comparison, the cane growers in Queensland and northern New South Wales did not do so badly. Most of the sugar produced was consumed within Australia, and the federal protective tariffs prevented sugar falling to the normal world price. The internal price was maintained until 1933 by the retention of the full tariff against much cheaper imported sugar; by that time, the worst of the depression was over and 35,000 men had kept their jobs.

One of the worst blows to the primary sector came from the federal government itself. James Scullin had brought Labor to power in Canberra in 1929, and was immediately confronted by the economic crisis and the fall by £80 million in the national income in his first year in office. Apart from the drop in world prices, British capital was withdrawn from Australia. The government's hands were tied. Whatever it wanted to do, it could not, simply because it had no way of finding the money. Labor had no answers to the problem, and they invited Sir Otto Niemeyer of the Bank of England to advise them.

The two matters to which Niemeyer drew attention were the artificial protection of Australian industry, including farming, and the heavy borrowing overseas which had taken place in the 1920s. His main argument was that Australia was not creating enough wealth to justify the standard of living which its people then expected. This is a situation which Australia has since failed to address since Niemeyer offered the diagnosis. As the first edition of this book was being published in 1986, the Australian dollar had plummeted against all the major world currencies, the country had borrowed heavily to sustain standards of living even though a major drought two years previously had slashed wheat production and there had been a falloff in mineral export prices. Of course, since then we have had the commodities boom of the first decade of the new century; however, once our mineral boom ends then we have once again the need to contemplate Niemeyer's strictures.

In 1985 (and again in 2011) the Federal government was able to put off the day of reckoning by means of the national deficit. Scullin had no such luxury. Closed in by the financial institutions, he came up with the idea that Australia could trade its way out of disaster. In March 1930 the Prime Minister spoke on the wireless. Scullin told the farmers of the nation that one of the remedies to the financial crisis which had beset Australia was to increase the exports of wheat and wool. It became known as the 'Grow More Wheat' campaign. He said that wheat growers were entitled to a guaranteed price, especially if they changed from wool to wheat production. Now, that was only what he wanted, but the men of land who listened to him or read his speech in the newspapers assumed that the federal government would definitely come to their aid by setting a minimum price. 'The wheat farmers have a golden opportunity to give the lead,' Scullin told them.

Give the lead they did.

After horsepower came steam and ploughing was a cumbersome business, as this photograph taken in Gippsland, Victoria, in 1886 illustrates.

National Library of Australia

In 1931 the farms of Australia yielded up 212 million bushels of wheat, a crop greater in volume than the wartime record harvest in 1915. The problem was that the Commonwealth Bank refused to lend the government the money to support the price of the wheat, and the Senate — which Labor did not control — would not pass a minimum price of four shillings to be paid for delivery of wheat at railway stations. That was the sum the House of Representatives had approved in the Wheat Advances Act; what the wheat grower got on average was one shilling and nine pence. The growers were now in total despair. They raged at public meetings but the game was up. There was nothing more to be done: many walked off their farms, never to return, and the wheatlands rang with the sound of auctioneers' hammers as mortgagees tried to recoup as much as they could. The wheat farmers had lost £22 million doing their bit to revive Australia. For those who stayed on their land, worse was to come. In the 1936-37 season, world prices shot up even though Australia's grain acreage was well down due to the ravages of the depression. The response, naturally, was to plough more land for wheat, and the result was an even bigger crop in 1937-38, by which time prices had fallen again and once more the wheat grower needed government assistance. The war brought many more problems, and then there was the 1944 drought. What was amazing was that by 1945 the Australian wheat grower had suffered a string of bitter blows since 1928, and yet most had the resilience and endurance to last.

What the depression underlined was that too much of Australia's cropping was uneconomic. In the early 1930s, nearly a third of the wheat farms were less than 100 acres in size, although it was seen in the previous chapter that 200 acres was regarded as the minimum economic crop. The average production cost on farms of less than 100 acres was three and two pence per bushel, far above the price prevailing at the depths of the depression. When many of these farmers inevitably went broke, the banks and other lenders found that too often the land and plant mortgaged fetched less than its value simply because there were so few buyers. The high hopes that had been held a few years previously made the disappointment all the more wretched and bitter.

The state governments did want to help farmers to stay on their land, if only to stop them moving to the city to join the ranks of the unemployed. South Australia was the first to act with its 1929 Debt Adjustment Act, but that was little help because it did not prevent creditors taking the ultimate action through the legal system. Western Australia passed similar legislation. In 1930 New South Wales passed the Moratorium Act, which dealt with interest owed on mortgages but not liens in the hands of the banks, of which there were many. New South Wales, among others, legislated in 1931 to provide farmers with advances to buy seed, without which they could not have planted a crop and, therefore, would have had even less chance of paying their debts. By 1935 the total indebtedness of the wheat growers was £150 million.

The wheat industry was still in poor shape when World War II began. While other sectors of primary industry had recovered, the wheat grower could not point to a year in the previous decade which could be classed as a good one.

The demands of World War II

The war saw the repetition of many of the headaches of 1914-18. In the 1939-40 season the wheat farms produced 210 million bushels. At the beginning, it seemed that this time most of the wheat would get to its overseas destination. For the first year the British had a good supply of merchant shipping, and their shortage of U.S. dollars encouraged them to buy what they could in the sterling area. But soon it was becoming difficult to move the crop, and it was again stacked (although there was not much damage by mice this time-something had been learned). Anyway, the British and Australian governments were more interested in wool; the London government wanted to buy the whole wool clip (except for that needed by Australian manufacturers) for the duration of the war, as they did in South Africa and New Zealand. The price they offered was well above that which prevailed in 1939 (the August sales that year having been cancelled as war approached). The British needed the wool and were prepared to provide the shipping necessary to collect it. By monopolising the production of the three dominions, the British government controlled a large part of the world's wool supply. Drought struck Western and South Australia and New South Wales in 1940-41, and the combination of that with the British demand for wool saw much wheat land converted to grazing pasture.

The British did not want Australian fresh fruit, nor much meat. With this general air of discouragement except to the wool grower, many of the younger farmers lost heart and joined the services, in which they were initially encouraged by the manpower committees. One of the few benefits of this period was that many wheat growers, in order to reduce production, began rotating land, interspersing clover each two or three seasons, a practice which helped restore soil fertility.

Then Japan bombed Pearl Harbor. And, by early 1942, there were 14,000 U.S. troops in Brisbane alone, thousands more in other parts of Queensland, other states and the Northern Territory. They needed food, but many farms had run down production. Anyway, the men they needed to help boost food output had gone off to war. The American influx and the threat of Japanese invasion meant that new industries were established to manufacture war materials. More men left the land as conscription came into force. The munitions factories needed labour, and these factories paid a great deal better than farm work. In the 1942-43 financial year more than 61,000 men left the rural labour force.

Life on the Australian farm in the thirties was still one of general privation and poor wages. It was no wonder that those who saw the chance of living on a good wage, in a decent house and having all the modern conveniences jumped at the chance of factory work. The situation became so serious that the federal authorities soon began to defer the call-up for farm workers or else the food production system would have completely broken down. There was a particular problem with sugar and fruit, as these depended for the harvest on seasonal labour, and a seasonal worker was hard to control. Many of the American soldiers used their leave to work on farms, particularly the cane farms in Queensland, simply to escape the cities bursting at the seams with their comrades. In late 1943 the government offered former farm workers both in the services and in essential secondary industries the opportunity to go back to the land. Few took up the offer. At the end of the war, in stark contrast to the mood of 1918, most of the troops who had come from rural occupations refused to go back when they were released from the services. They were now accustomed to something better, and saw the high wages in the cities as a way to maintain those standards and expectations.

The demand from the half million Americans who passed through Australia was so great that food rationing was introduced. A much greater problem was that the U.S. soldiers did not much like the food they were offered in Australia. The Americans did not like mutton, nor did they have much of a taste for all the pumpkin, onion, squash and turnips with which they were fed. They wanted green vegetables, tomatoes, potatoes and fruit. One of the interesting sidelights of the meeting of the two cultures was the American amazement that so many Australians, and particularly young women, had false teeth. Nor could the Australian girls believe that all the soldiers they met had their own teeth; one soldier at least found it disconcerting that his girlfriends in Brisbane would believe his teeth were his own only after trying to take them out with their hands.

The U.S. serviceman expected plenty of pork and bacon (pig meat being the one type of meat which the British also wanted to buy from Australia) and oranges and green vegetables, the fruit and vegetables which had never until then figured largely in the Australian diet. They insisted on plenty of whole milk but the dairy industry was particularly hard hit by labour shortages and those vegetables that could be grown all went to the U.S. mess halls. Australian civilians found that there were no oranges or bacon available to them, and that dairy products were in extremely short supply. The Americans did take over one farm to grow their own vegetables and operated a poultry farm to provide eggs, and several other Queensland properties were run by the Red Cross in an effort to meet American dietary demands.

Of course, the American servicemen wanted to take their food wherever they went in the Pacific, and there were also U.S. labour units in isolated parts of the continent which needed to be supplied, like the black battalions which were put to work to seal the Alice Springs to Darwin highway. In the years after the Pacific war began, canning of vegetables in Australia increased tenfold, processing of milk doubled and a new industry in dehydrated food began. The supply requirements were such that, even when food could be supplied from various parts of Australia, there were great problems in getting it to the Americans. The narrow gauge railway systems of Western Australia and Queensland and the rickety Central Australian Railway from Port Augusta to Alice Springs almost came to the point of organisational collapse.

Farmers were hampered by lack of superphosphate. Nauru and Ocean Island, which had been run by the Australians on behalf of their British and New Zealand partners in the phosphate enterprise, had been captured by Japanese forces. The nearest replacement source was the Middle East, but such was the cost and the problems in transporting it that it had to be both rationed and subsidised by the federal government.

One minor sector which did quite well out of the war was the tobacco-growing industry. It had been a small and practically unheard of crop as far as Australia was concerned before the war, but the demands for cigarettes not only in the forces but from the civilian population did not diminish even when there was a problem of supply. Before the war, most cigarettes and tobacco sold were made largely from imported leaf, but the shortage in Australia gave the growers a ready market, not. only for what they already produced, but for the increased production they undertook. Regulations required tobacco companies to use an increasing proportion of Australian leaf; by 1945 the requirement was up to 30 per cent.

Apart from the drought of 1944-45, the Australian farmer came through World War II fairly well. While most farms had been run down owing to shortage of farm materials during the war, the labour shortages had been partly a blessing in that the farmers' wages bills were reduced or eliminated. Many dairy farmers, for example, switched to beef production to cut down on the need for labour. The farmers had usually been able to sell all they produced, and while the profitability may not have been all that it would have been, at least the regulated war economy had cushioned the farmer from the worst of the fluctuations of the world market.

This farm in the Canberra area has moved into the age of tractors, but there is still plenty of hard manual toil involved.

National Library of Australia

The beginning of the war had seen the end of the pioneering era of Australian farming. The pioneer fringes of the land had all been taken up and there was not much left to do by way of settlement. Even the soldier settlement schemes after 1945 rarely involved new lands, but rather subdivision and resettlement of existing productive land. But there were challenges, nevertheless.

The main challenge was the quality of Australian farming, and the mental acceptance of the tariff mentality. Other countries were being more innovative: New Zealand, for example, was obtaining much higher dairy production per unit by concentrating on the quality of feed the cow was given, a concept not widely recognised in Australia in 1945. It was thought, rather, that breeding was all. Land management left much to be desired, as it had from early days of the settlement around Sydney. In 1945 the Dean of the Faculty of Agriculture at Melbourne University, Samuel Wadham summed up the challenge ahead:

Farmers must recognise that land ownership has responsibilities as well as rights and that it is incumbent on them to conserve their soils and raise the standard of farming so as to maintain soil fertility.

Chapter 11

The New Challenges

UNTIL THE LATE 1950s the produce of Australia's farms accounted for more than 80 per cent of the nation's exports. In 1972-73, the proportion of primary exports had fallen to just over half, and by 1982-83 agricultural and pastoral industries produced just a quarter of Australian export trade. In 2012, the Department of Foreign Affairs and Trade exports facts sheet does not mention primary products, listing only the big five — iron ore, coal, gold, crude petroleum and natural gas. Farm exports in value terms have tripled since 1974, but they're still dwarfed by the new pillars of the economy.

Overall, production has increased rather than fallen. Between 1949 and 1961, for example, the number of sheep in Australia increased by more than 60 per cent, while better pasture, more and better fertiliser and the end of the rabbit as a major pest allowed the Australian farmer to increase production across the board, interrupted only by natural disasters.

What has happened is that mining and industrial exports have boomed in recent decades, building on the foundations laid by the farmer to make Australia one of the most prosperous nations on earth. The 'glamour' mining stocks have replaced the farmer in public perception as the provider of the good times.

The period since the end of World War II has seen a dramatic change in the notion of farming held by Australians. When the Australian colonies celebrated the centenary of white settlement in 1888 about half of Australia's population lived outside the cities and was in direct connection with the land. The tie between city and country was strong, and before the development of a significant industrial base the farmers were recognised as a major force in the affairs of the colonies.

By the time of the bicentenary in 1988 it was all quite different. Not much more than five or six per cent of Australia's population now worked on farms, and few city dwellers had any contact with farms or farmers. A drought which resulted in the deaths of thousands of farm animals and the threat of economic ruin to parts of the countryside by the time made less impact in Sydney or Melbourne than a train strike which lasted a few days. Few metropolitan newspapers, radio or television stations had staff assigned to covering agricultural, pastoral or rural subjects.

The farmers had to make some dramatic gesture in order to find themselves in the limelight. Such was the case in the 1970s when disgruntled beef men, hit by a collapsed price, formed the Cattlemen's Union and presented a high profile by way of controversial statements and acts, including one grazier shooting his herd because it was not worth taking the animals to market.

If you live in a city and make no conscious effort to find out what happens beyond the Blue Mountains, the Dandenong Ranges, the Adelaide Hills, or wherever, you could be forgiven for thinking that farming was almost non-existent in Australia. In the 1980s it was only when there was a drought or a violent demonstration by Victorian dairy farmers — when, in other words, there was a bit of tragedy or drama which made for good pictures on the six o'clock news — that any acknowledgment was made in the city that there was another nation of Australians. It is an interesting comment that Australia is one of the few western democracies where the country and urban conservative voters have been represented by separate political parties, in the form of the National (formerly Country) Party and the Liberals.

The farmers' image may not have been helped by the continued reliance — when it suited — on government support and protection. In the post-war period, no better example is afforded than that of the wool-grower.

With the build-up and outbreak of the Korean War there was an enormous world demand for wool, primarily in the United States. The Korean winter can be bitter, and it was essential to stockpile the fibre for thick uniforms. From May 1949 until March 1951 the prices skyrocketed at the Australian wool sales, climbing nearly five-fold. At one stage wool fetched a pound in value per pound in weight, after which prices tumbled but still remained at a level 50 per cent higher than in early 1949. Enormous amounts of money flowed into Australia, and into New Zealand too. The Federal government, apart from imposing certain restrictions which ensured that farmers had to put some of the money aside for taxation purposes, suggested that a regulated marketing scheme be devised using the surplus income from this windfall to even out prices in the future, much as was being done with wheat.

The wool-grower would have none of it. The growers voted 63,740 to 16,310 to take their money and run, and in 1965 rejected a similar proposal for a reserve price scheme, although not by such a large margin.

There were some plausible arguments for a reserve price. Wool auction sales were notoriously unstable and unpredictable. Farmers never know in advance of a sale what the prices will be like, and prices offered could vary even within one day of a sale. But it was not until 1970 that the logic of this argument began to appeal to the wool-grower; that year prices fell to what they had been in 1946 and production costs were a great deal higher than a quarter of a century earlier. The growers appealed to the federal government for help, and the result was the reserve price as administered by the new Australian Wool Commission.

The wheat farmers had accepted stabilisation as early as 1948 after rejecting a continuation of the wartime controls which were a great deal more onerous than stabilisation. They had good crops in the five years after the war, including a 220 million bushel harvest in the 1947- 48 season. The problem was that in 1948 the world price fell, and the federal government offered to guarantee a price of six shillings and threepence on wheat delivered to ports for export, up to a total of 100 million bushels, the grower being taxed when the world price went above that in other years. The wheat grower was particularly susceptible to the suggestion: the fall of 30 per cent in the world price refreshed memories of the 1929-45 years of hardship.

In good years the wheat harvest has continued to burgeon. In 1967-68 about 26 million acres were planted in wheat, and the harvest that year was 467 million bushels. One outlet which helped wheat surpluses was the Chinese market. Even when Australia refused to recognise the Mao Tse-tung government in Peking, the anti-communist Federal government and farming lobby was more than anxious to do business there. The trade began in 1961 with the sale of one million tons of wheat, as well as quantities of barley and flour. Just as the Wool Commission introduced rationalisation into the annual sale of wool, so the Australian Wheat Board brought about orderly marketing of Australia's grain (although as the 21st century dawned the privatised AWB — as it was by the called — and the single-desk system were drawing plenty of criticism). The grain-handling authorities in each state looked after the wheat, the board sold it. The Wheat Board made substantial advance payments to farmers while the Federal government underwrote 95 per cent of exported returns as a guaranteed minimum price.

Unless world wheat prices tumbled significantly, by the later decades of the 20th century grain production could be expected to increase in Australia because technical developments had made possible both greater yields and the use of what were once marginal areas. This happened in New South Wales, where larger machines made it possible for growers be opportunistic and move quickly to plant and harvest crops in the years when the moisture levels made it feasible. Between 1971 and 1981 the area devoted to wheat in Western Australia almost doubled, but yields did not keep pace because some areas north of the wheat belt could be sown only every three or four years.

The white elephant that could (up to a point)

One of the more extraordinary schemes to bring in new land to production also took place in Western Australia. It was the Ord River irrigation scheme. As one commentator, Bruce Davidson, author of *The Northern Myth* , has put it, 'The most interesting aspect of the Ord River Irrigation Project is that anyone should at any time have thought that it would be economically viable'.

But how times have changed. Back in the mid1980s it was largely viewed as a white elephant. As this book's first edition in 1986 noted, "So far, it has cost more than $110 million of federal and state money, and precious little has been gained in return."

The scheme aroused the scepticism in many because it was long seen as just another episode in the recurring obsession with the supposed need to develop the north, that assumption previously noted being as based on two beliefs: one, that somewhere and somehow untold riches await; and, two, that if we did not do something about it, someone else (implicitly Asian) would, an idea reinforced by the Japanese attack on Australia the 1941-45 Pacific war. In the post-war years, further underlined by China falling to the communists, you can understand the vulnerability felt by many Australians. But, given that in the 1960s and onwards, there was ample evidence that agriculture in the far north could be conducted under restraints and constraints, it was surprising to many that the Federal government in Canberra was dragged into what was widely felt to be a fiasco adding up to the tune of many millions of dollars.

In the first decade of the 20th century, the Coalition government under then Prime Minister John Howard established the Northern Australia Land and Water Taskforce. When it reported in December 2009, the taskforce was of the opinion that, while there may have been opportunities for small-scale agricultural development in the far north, there were many barriers to widespread conversion of land. Those roadblocks included seasonal water limits, problems storing water, isolation from major population centres, reduced access to labour and skills, poor transport and other infrastructure, a lack of knowledge about appropriate farming methods and indigenous issues.

And yet we appear to have now gone full circle. In 2012, there was Prime Minister Julia Gillard in Kununurra getting involved in discussions about Australia's far north becoming a new "food bowl" for Asia. The Institute of Public Affairs was calling for building more dams in a region where some areas received almost double the rainfall of the Murray-Darling Basin. Just months earlier, the latest irrigation plan in East Kimberley had blown out by $102 million. This was part of the Ord East Kimberley Development Package financed by the Federal and West Australian governments; they provided $415 million between 2009 and 2012 to bring into production a further 8,000 hectares of agricultural land.

The idea that the Ord River could be developed had been kicking around since 1909 when Western Australia first investigated the possibilities of tropical agriculture. The subject was revived periodically over the years, always to be put aside for some reason. One of the main arguments against such development was that it probably would not work, and that the money would be far better spent on the south-western lands of Western Australia, which not only were capable of improvement in both agriculture and pastoral yields but comprised an area where the great majority of people had shown a preference to live.

The state government set up a small experimental farm on the Ord in 1941 but lasted barely four years. However, by 1958 it was an idea whose time had apparently come, with Canberra and Perth picking up the cost of building a dam at Kununurra.

By 1966, there were thirty-one irrigated farms. Then, by 1974, a second storage dam was full further up the Ord River and thus Lake Argyle came into existence. The "develop the North" concept was in full cry. All doubts — and many had been raised by critics of the scheme — were cast aside.

Huge public works schemes have a tendency to arouse in those who have proposed and supported them a need to continue to justify what they are doing. In 1965 the director of the northern development division of the federal Department of National Development delivered a paper in which he silently acknowledged that the Ord region might not produce all the crops which were expected of it, although initial studies had claimed that the area, once sufficient water was available, would be suitable for cotton, rice sorghum, maize, barley, wheat, oats, safflower, soybeans, sugar cane and pasture. As it turned out, only cotton was grown in viable quantities, and the official, Mr Rex Patterson, said in the paper that 'cotton production as a monoculture ... is a sound economic proposition even if the bounty is completely removed and the producers had to operate on the export price'. But the reality was a great deal different. The last cotton was harvested in 1975 — and there would be no more picked until 2011 when genetically-modified plants were grown.

The Ord scheme was seen as a follow-on to the Snowy River development which, apart from its hydro-electricity element, had increased irrigation potential along the Murray and Murrumbidgee rivers. At the same time, the Queenslanders were working on their Burdekin irrigation scheme. The first stage of the Ord scheme provided irrigation to 12,000 hectares, and then in 1967 the federal government agreed to provide another $48 million to bring stage two into being, to irrigate another 40,000 hectares. Charles Court, the state minister for the north-west, later premier, saw the scheme as promoting closer settlement, even though the Ord was 1,600 kilometres away, across semi-desert, from the main settlement areas of Western Australia.

The cotton growing had been able to survive as long as it did only because of the bounty paid by the Federal government; at one stage that bounty accounted for a third of the amount being received by the Ord farmers. Not only was there the bounty from Canberra, but help from Perth in the form of deferment of rental payments on the local cotton ginnery, subsidised ginnery power charges and low water rates.

The cotton was abandoned in the 1970s for several reasons. The major one was *Heliothis armigera*, a cotton pest which revelled in the cotton monoculture and the absence of predators. Insecticides not only had a diminishing effect on this pest as time passed, but the sprays were expensive to use in quantity, and the farmers already had the heavy cost of all the fertilisers which they found the Ord required. In fact, 16,000 grams per hectare of DDT was applied to control the pest. On top of that was the declining yield as the depredations of the insects increased, and the reduced quality of the cotton as a result of long exposure to sunlight.

In the end, like the soldier settlers forty years earlier, the cotton growers of the Ord River realised that they could never hope to pay off or even service the debts in which they had enmeshed themselves. Other crops and plans withered in the relentless sun of the north-west. Safflower was tried in 1963, but returns were so low the crop was not sown the following season. When rice was grown there was a high incidence of cracked grain, and it cost twice as much to grow as the rice crops of the Murrumbidgee Irrigation Area in New South Wales. M.I.A. rice, incidentally, already needed government economic protection, and had been expanded only when there was a specific need, in that case the demand for rice in World War II when most Asian supplies had been cut off. The Sydney-based Hooker Corporation tried fattening cattle on sorghum, but that soon stopped when the bottom fell out of beef prices.

By 2007, the Western Australian government was once again looking to cotton, concerned as it was that so dominating was the cultivation of sugar cane that this was also threatening to become a monoculture. Agriculture department experts recommended growing genetically-modified cotton to provide a rotation crop for sugar. Rotating cane, which is a grass, with cotton, a broad leaf crop, would — they argued — would help to prevent the build up of soil pests and diseases.

So, in late 2011, the first genetically-modified cotton was harvested in the Ord River irrigation area. The crop was modified for resistance to the moth species that had done all that damage back in the 1960s.

The problem for the Ord scheme during the first 50 years of its existence was the fact that it never promised to produce anything that could not be grown or bred in more temperate and accessible areas of Australia, and if it were to succeed and overcome the enormous inherent cost problems then it would be necessary for farms on the Ord River to produce much greater yields than other Australian farms.

In a move to try and find some economic justification for the project, the Western Australian Government in 1976 commissioned CSR (formerly the Colonial Sugar Refining Company) to report on the potential for sugar cane development on the Ord. In 1981, however, demand for land began to pick up, and it seemed that rice, sunflower, sorghum, soybeans and peanuts might be expanded. In 1982 the *West Australian* newspaper reported the existence of a new confidence regarding what mining millionaire Lang Hancock had called Australia's greatest white elephant.

By that time there were more than thirty farms producing two crops a year, and land prices were rising steeply. It was not before time, as by 1982 the state government had recouped a bare $3.5 million of the $15 million it had spent in the previous five years. By the mid-1980s the West Australians were talking about planting enough sugar cane to supply an ethanol plant on the Ord, which would produce 120 million litres of ethanol fuel a year. There has never been any shortage of ideas and plans where the Ord River has been concerned.

Now comes — once again — the "Asian food bowl" notion. But the world has changed. Asia is finding it increasingly hard to feed itself. By mid-2012 politicians in Canberra were riven by plans to develop northern Australia for agriculture using Chinese government investment to build irrigation schemes.

The farmer faces a changed world – and along came China

"Rural riches ahead" roared the front page of one farming newspaper in August 2012. Experienced economists, the paper said, predicted that the galloping growth of China and India would rub off on countries such as Australia.

China's lost of much of its arable land — pollution was one cause, but mainly due to urbanisation and industrialisation encroaching on farmland — and it was facing severe water shortages. And all while its population acquired the spending power to provide more and better food; the consumption of meat has exploded in China.

But there is always a downside in Australian farming. We became more and more dependent on some types of imported food. Figures for fiscal 2011 showed that Australia exported $446 million worth of fruit but imported $2 billion worth. Vegetable exports amounted to $313 million — but imports came to $651 million. The Australian consumer wants naval oranges year round (so they're brought from California in the off-season here) and asparagus, too (hence the sight of Thai and Peruvian asparagus in the shops).

The fortunes of Australian farmers have swung like a pendulum since the end of the 1939- 45 war. Setting aside droughts, there was the wool boom of the Korean War, the advent of the European Common Market and then its evolvement as the European Community, meant the loss of market share in Britain and the creation (as a result of subsidies) of huge surpluses—the so-called "butter mountain" and the "wine lake". Then in the 1980s there was an air of gloom hanging over the rural sector. As I wrote in 1986:

> The bottom line is that Australian farming —in many ways uneconomic for decades and for this reason supported by subsidies and protection —is now becoming unprofitable as well even with such support, a plight from which there appears to be no rescue in sight. Mice plagues and droughts are problems, but the real reasons for the decline in farming are more implacable.

By the mid-1980s, Australia had 30,000 fewer farming families than it did during the wool boom of the early 1950s. By that time, too, it was possible for the Australian Army to propose taking a large swathe of farming land in the central west of New South Wales for a firing range; that would have been unthinkable twenty or thirty years before, and was indicative of the status of farming as now viewed by the great majority of insulated city dwellers.

International competition seemed an insurmountable problem by the 1970s and 1980s . The European Community, by degrees of protection and subsidy which would make even past Australian governments blush guiltily, had produced huge agricultural surpluses. No longer was the British market a safe and sizable one for Australia. More than that, the European Community is in a situation where it can supply world markets with dairy products, beef, grain, sugar and wine at cheap prices with the community paying the European farmers the difference — dumping, in other words.

The Europeans and New Zealanders both then subsidised their dairy products to the point where their cheese sold in Australian supermarkets more cheaply than the real production cost in Australia. The result was a glut within Australia, so that the price for butterfat to Australian dairy farmers dropped by 40 per cent. At the same time costs were skyrocketing: in the first half of the 1980s, rates and taxes rose 70 per cent and interest rates by 80 per cent. Official statistics showed that by mid decade average farm income (all types of farms) was below $7,000. Dairy families were particularly hard hit, many of them earning below the minimum wage and significant numbers running their farms at a loss, meaning that they only plunge further into debt. But their choices are restricted; they usually have no other skills, and the country towns and even the main cities, with their already high rates of unemployment, have no jobs to offer these people.

Stories which echo the desperate years of the early selectors were starting to emerge in the 1980s. Men were driving trucks on interstate runs while the women are left to manage the dairying as best they can; or else the women found full — or part-time jobs —in the town, usually at quite low pay, while the men worked on the land and look after the children. Clothes were passed on for re-use and children were doing jobs that formerly would have been handled by a hired labourer.

Australian farming has had its downturns in the past, but they have been due mainly to climatic disasters or foreign economic downturns of short-term cyclical nature. Never before had nations produced mountains of unsaleable food, and fought each other to undercut prices on the world market.

Sugar is another salutary tale. The point was made in an earlier chapter that the cane-grower has rarely been viable in the Australian north without state aid of some type. But the sugar industry was left gasping when, between 1981 and 1985, the world price fell by 90 per cent. In 1981 the world price was thirteen U.S. cents a kilogram; by 1985 it was 1.36 cents, with every indication that it would drop even further. As before, other main producers subsidised production, the United States and the countries of European Community being in the forefront. It was demonstrated yet again that using highly-paid white labour means that sugar cannot compete without subsidy with the cheaper production in the underdeveloped countries. And, as Australia exports four-fifths of its sugar, it has been particularly hard hit by the price drop. If growers had to walk off their land and those remaining were to be supported by the domestic market, many of the mills would be forced to close with devastating effect on the Queensland towns which have grown up around the mills.

The Canberra-based Bureau of Agricultural Economics has predicted low world prices for primary commodities for the remainder of this century. What seems inevitable is the amalgamation of holdings as more large companies move into agribusiness, the family farmer replaced by the farm manager backed by his employer's capital resources. (About a third of Australian pastoralists who sold out over the last decade did so because of bankruptcy.) It is a trend which is taking place in all developed economies, most notably in the United States, where the Reagan administration in 1985 let it be seen that the American government would no longer protect the smaller farmers from going out of business.

Yet, Australian agriculture became the most efficient it had ever been. Between 1955 and 1975 primary production almost doubled. The difficulty was that prices slumped in real terms. By the mid-1980s, wool fetched (again in real terms) about a sixth of what it did in 1950, mutton a quarter, wheat only little more than a third, and while beef maintained its relative price, it was the one area where production dropped, as a result of reductions in beef herds.

So that when drought or other natural disasters strike, those on the land have fewer reserves with which to withstand the economic blow. In 1985, primary producers who had still not recovered from the appalling 1979-83 drought were being confronted with another big dry spreading through Queensland and New South Wales.

Just as insidious for the country's rural future is the threat from land speculation and subdivision in farming land. In New South Wales alone, the state Department of Agriculture estimated that between 1970 and 1979 592,000 hectares or 1.5 million acres were lost to farming. That constituted about 2.5 per cent of Australia's prime farming land. Since then, further tracts of highly fertile land used to grow vegetables for Sydney has disappeared under housing sub-divisions.

The greatest pressure on land during the post-war years was from the hobby farmer: of the above land lost in 1970-79, 95 per cent of it was due to subdivision into hobby holdings. Urbanisation took 4.2 per cent and mining 0.7 per cent. Subdivision of farming land is a continuous process throughout the nation, but the areas under greatest pressure are the north coast of New South Wales and the south-east corner of Queensland, the Adelaide Hills in South Australia and the countryside fanning out from Canberra where some of Australia's best grazing land has been cut up for weekend retreats for workers in the Australian Capital Territory. Subdivision causes problems other than just loss of productive land. Many owners visit their new hobby farms only a few times each month, and while they are busy at work in town the weeds spread and the sheep get lice. A specific case was reported to the New South Wales Legislative Council in 1975 where a block of land at Mudgee was subdivided into ten hectare lots, none with electricity or water connected. Noxious weeds such as St John's wort and Bathurst burrs were a problem, as were unmended fences and the consequent straying by stock.

The Adelaide Hills is a major agricultural area of South Australia but by the mid-1980s hobby farmers there outnumbered full-time primary producers by two to one. This sort of development has a domino effect, because the existing farmers cannot afford to increase the size of their farms owing to the inflated values caused by subdivision, and they are then tempted to sell out and make a good profit themselves, their land going the way of the former neighbours'. A study in the Cudgen area of northern New South Wales showed that a typical forty acre property which cost $30,000 in 1970 was worth $450,000 in 1980, with rates rising on the land in the decade by 60 per cent.

Prime farmland has also been under threat from erosion and salinity. Victoria's former Soil Conservation Authority estimated that 100,000 hectares of land in the state have been salt affected since white settlement. Altogether nearly 400,000 hectares of Australian farming land was at one stage threatened by salinity, a condition brought about when the water tables are altered either by irrigation or removal of tree cover. The irrigation salinity is located mainly on either side of the Murray River, into which much of the salt water drains. At Wakool, on the New South Wales side of the river, the state government at one stage was confronted by the threat of salinity covering 47,000 hectares. Before 1934 the land was used by several holdings for dryland sheep pasture. Then in that year the water was brought in, and land use became a mixture of rice, pastures and wheat. Several families became 400 families living on this piece of land.

In 1956 the first problems were noticed. The land was salting up, stunting plant growth. In 1963 drains were cut across the land to try and remove some of the salty sludge. By the mid 1970s six farms had been abandoned and laid waste. The land looked and felt as if it had been covered by sump oil, the trees had died and grass disappeared.

But hope springs eternal: in 2012, the Australian Centre for Plant Functional Genomics in Adelaide made a breakthrough, finding the answers to how rice becomes salt-tolerant. The centre believed this could lead to developing varieties of both rice and barley that could grow in saline conditions.

Then there was the big rabbit breakthrough. One of the reasons production soared in good seasons by the latter decades of the 20th century was the partial defeat of the rabbit by the virus disease myxomatosis. The first trials were held in 1950, and by late 1951 the disease had spread along the Murray River, up the Murrumbidgee and Lachlan systems, and to the south coast of Victoria and then into the highlands of New South Wales. Within a few years the rabbit was almost wiped out.

The one animal the farmer now does have occasion to kill is the kangaroo, a situation which has caused much protest from animal protection groups in the cities. Before the land was closely settled kangaroos were not such a problem; their opportunistic breeding patterns were such that in times of drought not only did the joeys and young kangaroos die first but the females stopped breeding. Then came the white farmers. Watering holes in inland New South Wales beyond the Darling River could once have been 100 kilometres or more apart, but now it is more likely to be ten kilometres. Landowners have provided the food and water to sustain the kangaroo population in times of drought, and the marsupials compete with sheep and cattle for what grazing land there is. The farmers, by shooting the kangaroos or engaging professional hunters, have aroused anger in some quarters, but they have little choice if they are to try and keep their stock alive.

We've also seen more diversification in recent decades. Some canegrowers experimented with other crops, while in Tasmania, for example, orchardists began been growing oils which will go into flavouring and perfumes. Trial crops have shown that peppermint, spearmint, fennel, parsley, boronia, pyrethrum and blackcurrant do well in the island state's soils. Tasmanian growers had already succeeded in growing poppies. The island now has a body called Essential Oils of Tasmania.

And just look at how Australians have produced world quality olive oils.

Figures produced by the National Farmers' Federation show there are now "approximately 134,000 farm businesses in Australia, 99 per cent of which are family owned and operated. Each Australian farmer produces enough food to feed 600 people, 150 at home and 450 overseas. Australian farmers produce almost 93 percent of Australia's daily domestic food supply. As of 2010-11, there are 307,000 people employed in Australian agriculture. The complete agricultural supply chain, including the affiliated food and fibre industries, provide over 1.6 million jobs to the Australian economy."

In fiscal 2011, Australia's farm and fisheries food production was $40.7 billion; of that meat was worth $13.6 billion, grains and oilseeds $12.2 billion, fruit and vegetables $7.4 billion and milk $3.9 billion. On top of that, food processors' output topped $82 billion.

The years ahead — like the ones behind us — are bound to be difficult, characterised at times by low prices, inflationary costs and the threat of drought.

Demanding more and more government aid is not the answer in the long term. After all, if the small businessman in the city makes the wrong decision and goes bust be does not expect the government to come to his aid, even though he may employ ten or more people. Why, the city-dwelling taxpayer might ask, should the farmer who produces something the market does not want be shown any further favours? In fact, the experience in both Europe and New Zealand has clearly demonstrated that subsidies and guaranteed purchase only encourage the people on the land to go on producing the same thing because they know that they will be paid for it. There may come a time when the farmer will have to accept walking off his land just as the industrialist has to close the factory doors if the business cannot sustain further losses.

The nation cannot, and should, not turn its back on the farmer. Help should be given to diversify, experiment, make more efficient and less costly the primary sector, so that the agriculturalists and pastoralists can adjust and survive. Their products will support a large part of the Australian economy and the standard of living which most Australians have come to take for granted.

The threats to the mill towns of Queensland and the dairying centres of Victoria which began to emerge in the mid 1980s were the first but certain signs that if the farmer goes down, the rest of us will go down with him.

Bibliography

Andrews, J., *Frontiers and Men*, Cheshire, Melbourne 1966

Atkinson, James, *An Account of the State of Agriculture and Grazing in New South Wales*, James Cross, London 1826

Battye, J.S., Western Australia: *A History from its Discovery to the Inauguration of the Commonwealth*, Oxford, London 1924

Bell, A.F., *The Story of the Sugar Industry in Queensland*, UQP, Brisbane 1956

Bennett, M.M., *Christison of Lammermoor*, Rivers, London 1928

Boldrewood, R., *Old Melbourne Memories*, Macmillan, London 1899

Bonwick, J., *Romance of the Wool Trade*, Griffth Farrar Okedon and Walsh, London 1887— *First Twenty Years of Australia*, Sampson Low Marston Seale and Rivington, London 1882

Boswell, Annabella, *Some Recollections of My Early Days*, undated

Brodribb, W.A., *Recollections of an Australian Squatter*, John Woods, Sydney 1883

Bromby, Robin, *The Country Railway in Australia*, Cromarty, Sydney 1983

Browne, C.W., *Overlanding in Australia*, Mason Firth & Co, Melbourne 1868

Buchanan, Gordon, *Packhorse and Waterhole*, Angus & Robertson, Sydney 1933

Bushell, N.K., *Australia for the Emigrant*, Cassell, London 1913

Butlin, S.J., *War Economy 1939-42*, Australian War Memorial, Canberra 1955

Campbell, W.S., *From Colony to Commonwealth*, NSW Department of Agriculture, Sydney NSW 1901.

Chauncey, W.S., *How to Settle in Victoria*, Slater Williams and Hodgson, Melbourne 1855.

Clark, C.M.H., *A History of Australia*, Melbourne University Press, Melbourne 1968 (and subsequent volumes)

Clarke, T., *Marriage at 6 a.m.*, Gollancz, London 1934

Colebatch, H.P., *Story of a Hundred Years,* Government Printer, Perth 1929

Collier, James, *The Pastoral Age in Australasia*, Holcombe & Tombs, London 1911

Collinson, J.W., *Early Days of Cairns*, W.R. Smith and Paterson, Brisbane 1939

Cotton, A.J., *With the Big Herds in Australia*, Watson Ferguson & Co, Brisbane 1931

Crawford, J.G., et al, *Wartime Agriculture in Australia and New Zealand*, Stanford University Press, California 1954

Curr, E.M., *Recollections of Squatting in Australia*, G. Robertson, Melbourne 1883

Dangar, H., *Index and Directory of the River Hunter*, James Cross, London 1828

Davidson, B.R., *The Northern Myth*, Melbourne University Press, Melbourne 1965 — *Lessons from the Ord*, Centre for Independent Studies, Sydney 1982

Davis, E.D., *Life and Times of Steele Rudd*, Lansdowne, Sydney 1976

De Satge, Oscar, *Pages from the Journal of a Queensland Squatter*, Hurst and Blackett, London 1901

Docker, Edward., *The Blackbirders: South Sea Labour*, Angus & Robertson, Sydney 1970

Donovan, Peter., *A Land Full of Possibilities*, UQP, Brisbane 1981

Easterby, H.T., *The Queensland Sugar Industry*, Queensland Bureau of Sugar Exporting Stations, Brisbane 1933

Eden, C.H., *My Wife and I in Queensland*, Longman Green, London 1872

Fletcher, B.H., *Landed Enterprise and Penal Society*, Sydney University Press, Sydney 1976

Foley, J.C., *Droughts in Australia*, Australian Bureau of Meteorology Bulletin No. 43, Melbourne 1957

Gregory, J.W., *Menace of Colour*, Seeley Service & Co, London 1925

Hamilton, George, *Experiences of a Colonist Forty Years Ago*, J. Williams, Adelaide 1880

Harris, W.K., *Outback in Australia*, H.W. Harris & Son, Newcastle 1913

Haygarth, H.W., *Recollections of Bush Life in Australia*, John Murray, London 1848

Hind, Cora, *Seeing for Myself*, Macmillan, Toronto 1937

Irvin, Eric, *Early Inland Agriculture*, Eric Irvin, Wagga Wagga 1962

Irwin, F.C., *The State and Position of Western Australia*, Simpkin Marshall & Co, London 1835

Kelly, J.H., *Struggle for the North*, Australasian Book Society, Sydney 1966

Kelly, W.J., *Rural Development in South Australia*, Rigby, Adelaide 1962

Kennedy, E.B., *Four Years in Queensland*, Edward Stanford, London 1870

Kent, Thomas, *A Letter to Barron Field Esq.*, London 1824

Kiddle, Margaret, *Men of Yesterday*, Melbourne University Press, Melbourne 1961

Matthews, James, *The Rabbit Pest in Australia*, The Speciality Press, Melbourne 1921

Peck, H.H., *Memories of a Stockman*, Stockland Press, Melbourne 1942

Powell, J.M., *The Public Lands of Australia Felix*, Oxford, Melbourne 1970

Roberts, S.H., *History of Australian Land Settlement*, Melbourne University Press, Melbourne 1924 — *The Squatting Age in Australia*, Melbourne University Press, Melbourne 1935

Scott, Ernest, *Australia During the War*, Angus & Robertson, Sydney 1936

Southey, Thomas Rise, *Progress and Present State of Colonial Sheep and Wools*, Smith Elder & Co, London 1851

Sutton, G.L., *The Invention of the Stripper*, Western Australian Journal of Agriculture, Perth 1937

Tolchand, Clifford, *The Humble Adventurer*, Lansdowne, Sydney 1965

Trollope, Anthony, *Australia and New Zealand*, Chapman and Hall, London 1876

Tyrwhitt, W.S., *The New Chum in the Queensland Bush*, J. Vincent, London 1888

Wadham, S.M., *Australian Farming 1788-1965*, Cheshire, Melbourne 1967

Wakefield, E.G., *A Letter from Sydney*, James Cross, London 1829

Walker, Thomas, *A Month in the Bush of Australia*, James Cross, London 1838

Waltham, E., *Life and Labour in Australia*, Henry J. Drane, London 1910

Waterson, D.B., *Squatter, Selector and Storekeeper*, Sydney University Press, Sydney 1968

West, John, *The History of Tasmania*, Henry Dowling, Launceston 1852

Wheelhouse, Frances, *Digging Stick to Rotary Hoe*, Cassell, Melbourne 1966

Williams, D.B., *Agriculture in the Australian Economy*, Sydney University Press, Sydney 1967

Robin Bromby has been a journalist and author for more than 50 years. *"The Farming of Australia"* is the first book released as a PDF, download at **www.highgatepublishing.com.au**.

Other titles by Robin Bromby:

"German Raiders of the South Seas" the story of the World War I merchant raiders Emden, Wolf and Seeadler and the threat they posed to Australia and New Zealand.

"Australian Railways: Their Life and Times" All the great (and terrible trains), the gauge nightmare, and the building of Australia as lines spread out into the country.

To be advised of these titles, get on the mail list at: **info@highgatepublishing.com.au**